Winner Take All

A Woman Exposes the Violation of Men's Rights at the Hands of Family Law

Molly Murphy, RN, CPMHN(c)

Legal Disclaimer

This book is written based on the experiences of the Author and expresses the Author's feelings. It is sold with the understanding that the Author is not engaged in rendering legal or other professional services by publishing this book. The Author disclaims any liability, risk, or loss that is a consequence, directly or indirectly, of the use and application of any of the contents of this book. The names and identifying characteristics of the people and situations in this book have been changed to protect the individual's privacy. This book is based on a true story.

First published by Dog Ear Publishing
4010 W. 86th Street, Ste H
Indianapolis, IN 46268
www.dogearpublishing.net

ISBN: 978-160844-380-2

This book is printed on acid-free paper.

Printed in the United States of America

ACKNOWLEDGMENTS

I would first like to thank Angelo Paino for editing this book during its development prior to publication. It is because of your tireless efforts that people will do more than simply read this book but will, in fact, "experience" it.

This book could never have been written without the help of people like Jeremy Swanson, Bob Hebblethwaite, Kris Titus, and Mary Lou Ambrogio. You are all pioneers in your efforts to promote change within our family law system.

Thanks to Barbara Kay from the *National Post* for her endorsement of this book, and for her continued support within the media for equal shared parenting.

To all the men, women, and children who contacted me over the last year after I appeared on the Tom Young radio show: Your words gave me the drive I needed to keep going until the final sentence was written.

Thanks to Tom Young for giving me access to a microphone from which I could speak the truth.

Thanks also to Patrick Portelance and Dave Nash for your efforts, through the creation of an upcoming documentary on family law and running across Canada, respectively, to bring public awareness to the fact that every child needs a father's guidance and love in his or her life. I applaud you!

To my family who stood by me and never complained while I worked night and day to complete this book: I love you!

To Adam, Rick and Bill: Please know that your suffering at the hands of family law was not in vain. Your pain is the passion that keeps us all fighting for equality.

And finally, thank you, God, for never allowing me to feel comfortable with injustice.

INTRODUCTION

It was never my intention to write this book. But then again, getting divorced wasn't on my "to do" list either. My background is in nursing and management, with twenty years of experience in these areas. My goal for going into nursing was simple; I wanted to help people. The goal has never changed, only my focus. I have family law to thank for that.

My core values have always been those of fairness and equality, whether making a decision in a healthcare setting or buying a chocolate bar for my kids. I live by this one rule: "What you do for one, you do for all."Unfortunately, in my experience, family law doesn't share my values. Divorce propelled me into a world where the core values are greed and excess, along with a "take what you want because you'll get it anyway" attitude. In this world, lawyers act more like coaches, training their female students on what to say and how to act to secure victory in court.

This book pulls back the veil of secrecy. You will learn the truth about what really happens when the door closes and the ex-wife and her lawyer begin to plan their strategy. Listen as the lawyer begins to describe the "financial buffet" that is there for the taking. Learn how easily a woman can gain custody of a child or turn a father's child against him through the process known as parental alienation. Listen in on all the private conversations that feminists, lawyers, and ex-wives often deny ever take place.

But this book is also about raw human emotion. You will become an intimate part of the lives of three men I care deeply about whom I witnessed going through divorce firsthand. Observe these men as they struggle to avoid the pitfalls that family law has in store for them: poverty, bankruptcy, alienation from their children, and even death. Feel what a father feels when he is denied access to the child he loves or is forced to give his last dollar to an ex when he can't eat or pay his own bills. Learn why lawyers, judges, and politicians are forced to cater to feminist groups. Read the suicide note left by a man who had everything taken away from him because of a court order.

This book is a labour of love. For eighteen months, I spent every evening and weekend at my computer writing the truth. During this time, if I wasn't writing or at work, I was responding to the hundreds of e-mails sent to me each week by fathers begging me to help them make sense of the insanity they were drowning in.

This book is my reply to their pleas. I wish that I could tell each man's story, as this book only scratches the surface of their struggles. It is my hope that this book is the catalyst in creating awareness worldwide regarding the discrimination that men face surrounding the issue of divorce. This book is not just for men. If you have an open mind, a desire for change, and intolerance for injustice, this book is for you.

CHAPTER ONE

I must have sat in my car facing the front door of that Paralegal office for over an hour. I couldn't come to the realization that once I walked through that door, my life was never going to be the same. I'd overcome every obstacle that life had put in front of me. I had to admit that I possessed a good ego, not an over-inflated one, but a healthy one. I always got any job I applied for, and I was a damn good psychiatric nurse. I could solve anyone's problems.

As I sat alone in the front seat of my car, however, I couldn't find an answer as to why my marriage had fallen apart. There was no article or psychiatric study to help me understand how my life had come to this point. My life was in total chaos. There was no white knight in shining armour rushing in to save the day. My idea of the fairy-tale marriage with the white picket fence was over.

As I stepped out of my car and slowly walked towards the door, I began to be consumed with guilt. I pulled the door handle with hesitation, knowing that once it opened, I would be admitting defeat for the first time in my life. I stepped into the reception area, and reality hit me like a cold slap in the face. I was getting divorced. My marriage was over. There was no turning back. No simple little kiss-and-make-up scenario was going to solve this problem. The wounds within our marriage had become too deep. This was not a game, like Monopoly. There was no passing Go, no collecting two hundred dollars, or simply packing up the game if you got tired of it. This was my new reality, and I didn't like it.

I had reluctantly entered into the game called divorce. I knew from past experience that it was a cruel game filled with misery, family destruction, and financial ruin. I had watched my cousin Rick and best friend Bill play this game before me. They both swore that greedy lawyers fuelled it. They had found that, on the surface, the lawyers would appear to have their best interests at heart, but the underlying motive, in their opinion, was to create as much anger and conflict between the two combatants as possible. More conflict would turn into more billable hours for the lawyers involved and a bigger paycheque in the end. In their opinion lawyers were the only winners, and being ethical did not seem part of their rules.

I stood there, filled with fear and anxiety, looking around that old weather-beaten office. I began to doubt that I could follow through with this. What fate now awaited me? Would I now be forced to endure the same suffering and heartache that both Rick and Bill had gone through? I began to feel pangs of nausea. Before I could turn around and bolt, the front desk receptionist noticed me and asked for my name. "I'm Molly Murphy. I'm here for an appointment with Mary."

"She's running late with another client, but if you sit down and fill out these forms, she'll be with you shortly."

I sat down and tried to focus on the questions on the forms. My mind began reeling, and I was overcome with sadness. Tears spilled out like rain onto the pages in my lap. All I could think of at that moment were my children.

Had I been selfish? Had I put my need to escape a failing marriage ahead of their needs? The words "if only" were pounding so loudly in my head that it became nearly unbearable. Had I ruined my children? Had I destroyed their ability to grow up healthy, happy, and well adjusted? Every child needs a father and a mother's love. I knew that firsthand. Both of my parents had passed away by the time I was barely a teenager. Not a day goes by that I don't think of them. What would my three daughters think of their parents once they reached adulthood? Would they still talk to both of us?

Talking problems out was what I had always preached to my children. Communication was the key. What sort of example was I now being to them? I felt like a hypocrite. I tried once again to answer the questions on the forms, but it was a lost cause. I couldn't have cared less about questions addressing who had brought what possessions into the marriage or who made more money. My mind was relentless; it simply wouldn't let my thoughts stray from my children.

Sitting back with eyes closed and fatigued from days and nights without food or sleep, I replayed the same scenario in my mind. I saw my three daughters sitting across from my husband and I, huddled together on the couch, as if giving each other comfort for the heartache that was about to come.

I can never erase the memory of the look of loss and hopelessness on their faces as we broke the news to them. After we announced that we were getting a divorce, no one had spoken for what seemed like an eternity. I knew that all the children had questions, but it was as if their collective voices had been paralysed. They were all gripped by fear of change, and as a family, we were traumatized. It was horrible. With one sentence, all of the laughter and joy that had once filled our home was replaced by silent tears, shed behind closed bedroom doors. A deathly silence now filled the house–a silence like one would sense walking through a battlefield littered with dead soldiers.

I glanced around the reception area and realized that I was the only person seated there. A sense of isolation and loneliness hit me in that instant. In my present state, I began to catastrophize my future. I wasn't worried about surviving financially, because I had a good job. I did wonder if I would ever love again or at least find someone I could share my golden years with. Many years had passed since I had gotten married, yet in my heart, it had been only yesterday that I had said "I do" to my husband.

Should we have done more marriage counselling? Should I have been a better wife and mother?

One unanswered question simply led into another. I was now on a journey that I would never wish for anyone. My soul ached for the past yet was filled with tears for the present.

As I waited to see Mary, I tried passing time by flipping aimlessly through the pile of old magazines scattered in front of me. Still, nothing could help me escape the hold that my mind had on my children. If I tried to read an article, a mental picture of them would fill my thoughts, and tears would begin to flow. I knew that no matter how old my girls were, they would always be my babies. I wanted to protect them so badly from all of this, but I didn't know how.

As the tears started yet again, I quickly made my way to a small bathroom located in the back of the office. The mirror exposed the toll that divorce was taking on my health. My eyes were puffy and sore from crying; they looked bloodshot and tired. I pulled some makeup from my purse and attempted to give myself some much-needed colour. I felt hungry, yet I couldn't eat. I was exhausted, yet I couldn't sleep. I had never felt this unhealthy in all my life. "For God's sake, keep it together. You're a Murphy!" I scolded myself as I looked into the mirror. Before leaving the bathroom, I stopped for a moment. "Dig deep, Molly. Show courage." With that mental pep talk under my belt, I took a deep breath, focused on the meeting to come, and headed back into the reception area.

I headed for the water cooler by the front door. I thought a little water in my stomach would help it settle before I went in to talk with the paralegal. I quickly gulped two cupfuls. The water felt soothing on my parched throat, but it also served to re-aggravate my nausea.

The water cooler was located under a big picture window. I stood there for a moment and watched the traffic go by, waiting for my stomach to settle. I wondered if any of those people driving by could be one life event away from standing where I was now and if they realized that anyone's life can change forever in the blink of an eye. A few days before, I had been just like them, rushing through my life, going nowhere fast, and always behind schedule. I had always been focused on what I had to get done and not on what really mattered. If any one of them knew that they were on the verge of losing their family or marriage forever, would they care if they missed a business meeting or skipped a few errands?

Divorce was definitely teaching me one thing–life was all about love. It was about valuing the relationships of those around you. It was about putting family first. Never take anything or anyone for granted. So what had I done wrong? Had I missed something obvious to my friends and family? Were these pangs of nausea really feelings of guilt? I'm not a stupid person. I knew that my marriage wasn't perfect. Whose is? I had known that there was trouble in paradise, so to speak, but I had never envisioned this–not my husband suddenly, without warning, telling me it was over, telling me that he simply couldn't do this anymore.

In my heart, I wished that there had been another woman, an affair or some type of abuse. I needed a reason to hate him. I wanted to get angry with him, but I couldn't. In fact, he was a good person, and I had nothing bad to say about him.

I did, however, need to somehow rationalize this divorce in my head. Two people who had simply fallen out of love and into friendship and then slowly drifted apart....that was the most plausible answer my mind could accept. Any other explanation was too painful to comprehend.

I decided a change in scenery might be good, so I sat down in a chair to the right of the window. I relished the sunshine as it streamed through the glass and bathed my body and face. It was the first time in days that I had felt warm. Enveloped in that blanket of warmth, I began to finally succumb to the fatigue I had been battling over the last few days. My body was shutting down. I kept fighting my urge to sleep. I needed to be alert for my meeting.

Still alone in the reception room, I thought a quick catnap couldn't hurt. I gently tilted my neck back and rested my head on the wall behind my chair. As my eyes began to close, I hoped that sleep would finally give me some respite. I was wrong.

Drifting in and out of consciousness, thoughts continued to flash through my mind at lightning speed. I began to dream of how difficult it would be at my age to rebuild my life, but I knew that I had no choice. I dreamed of how much I loved my children and how I would do anything to keep them safe and their lives as normal as possible. I felt happy in my dream state because I could see that I only wanted the best for everyone around me. That included my soon-to-be-ex-husband. I would never hurt him. I simply couldn't live with that kind of guilt. I thought of how different I was from many of the women I knew, in that I put no value on material possessions. My happiness had, and always would, come from within. Even in sleep, my one goal was to make this divorce process fair and equitable for everyone involved. I was just getting comfortable when I was abruptly drawn back into my ongoing nightmare.

"Mrs. Murphy, are you awake?" The receptionist shook my shoulder gently as she waited for me to respond. I slowly opened my eyes and brought her into focus. I was still a bit disoriented as she motioned me to get up and follow her down the hall.

"Please follow me," she said in a businesslike voice. "We are ready for you now."

CHAPTER TWO

I followed slowly down the hallway behind the receptionist, trying to come to terms with how my life had come to this. She motioned me into the first room on the left and asked me to have a seat. "Mary will be with you momentarily. I just have to give her your file." I was once again left to ponder my situation and what was yet to come.

The room was very small, cold, sterile-looking and sparsely furnished. No family pictures or even plants were evident–just an old boxy-looking outdated computer sitting alone on top of a scratched-up oak desk. The room was quiet except for the continuous click-clack sound of an old photocopier working overtime in the reception area and the drone of the minute hand slowly inching its way around the clock face on the wall behind me.

As I sat and stared at the wall behind the oak desk, my mind again escaped into memories of happier times. For a brief moment, I was reliving sights, sounds, and smells of everything and anything from the past....children's birthday parties, the patching up of scraped knees, the smell of Christmas turkey cooking in the oven, and even the clinking of wine glasses on my wedding day. No memory was insignificant. I saw my girls growing up from babies into young adults in a split second. The glue that held these memories together was the happiness and joy I felt as I recalled them. Would my life now be reduced to simply reflecting on a lifetime of memories? I was in a very dark emotional place. I knew that I was probably just overreacting to my situation, but trauma has a way of altering your perception of the world around you.

Someone knocked on the door. I quickly turned to see a short, stocky woman standing in the doorway. She stared directly at me as she spoke.

"Did I wake you? I'm your legal adviser. My name is Mary."

"I guess you caught me daydreaming," I said awkwardly. I attempted to put a smile on my face to let her know that I was acknowledging her attempt at humour. She leaned over and shook my hand firmly before sitting down at the computer. I could see only the top of her head as she hunched down in front of her keyboard and began to work.

Mary spent the first few minutes feverishly clicking information off my intake forms into the computer. I sat silently and waited for her to speak. The minutes felt like hours as she continuously punched numbers into her calculator. Finally, she let out a huge sigh and said, "That should about do it." With that, she moved her chair to the middle of the desk so we could now talk face-to-face. I could tell by her body language that she was friendly, yet very businesslike, and anxious to get right to the point. She was no amateur at this game. I was about to get a lesson on divorce that I would never forget. Mary opened our conversation with a very general question.

"What can I do for you, Molly?" she said in a very professional voice.

"I'm not sure,"I said sheepishly. "I don't honestly know what I'm doing here, other than the fact that my friends told me I should come." I may have been naïve, but I had always thought that legal advisors were only needed when two people can't agree about something serious on their own, or aren't really getting along.

"In truth, my ex and I are very good friends. We just don't make great marriage partners. We have a great deal of mutual respect for each other, and we love our children equally. Our marriage just kind of broke down. No abuse. No infidelity. I guess it's probably pretty boring as far as breakups go. In fact, before coming here, my ex and I sat down over coffee and worked out our own parenting plan, asset divisions, and a financial plan that we could both live with. I guess your job is basically done on this one. I've written everything down on a sheet of paper. It's here in my purse. If you war :, I can leave the details with you, Mary. You can write up the divorce agreement, and then we will both come in next week and sign all the papers." As I reached into my purse to get the paperwork, Mary leaned across the desk and touched my hand.

"That won't be necessary", she said.

"But I thought I could save you some valuable time, Mary," I explained. "I know that you are very busy. How can you write everything up if you don't have all the details?"

Mary leaned back in her chair and looked at me with a playful grin on her face.

"Did I say or do something wrong?" I asked inquisitively, not quite understanding why she was just staring at me.

"My dear Molly, you really don't have any clue as to how the family law works, do you?"

"I guess not," I said, unsure of what was coming next.

"It's my duty to explain to you what your rights are as a mother with three children, and also what you are financially entitled to within the family law system." Mary's demeanour was now becoming more relaxed. I could tell that she was about to give me the speech that she had given to many women before. Her body language conveyed that she was quite sure I would enjoy what she was about to tell me.

"If you listen to me carefully, Molly, and follow my advice, you will be well taken care of in the future."

I didn't know it yet, but she was about to tell me what was being served on today's "financial buffet table." I'd promised myself that I wouldn't hurt my ex in any way during the divorce process, but I had to admit that her last comment tweaked my interest. I listened with some reluctance as Mary proceeded to tell me how and what the legal system would take from my ex-husband, on my behalf, simply because I had married him.

"According to my calculations, you are entitled to about eight hundred dollars per month child support for you and your three girls. I arrived at this figure using government tables, based on his gross income, before taxes, of roughly forty thousand dollars per year. You are allowed to obtain his completed tax return each year. If his gross income changes, so do your payments. But don't worry, as there is some good news here. The more he makes, the more money you get, and there is no upper limit to these tables. Your ex-husband will have to make these payments until each one of your children reaches eighteen years of age and then, quite possibly, until they finish their post-secondary education. The best part here is that he pays all the tax on this money. The money is tax free in your hands, and he can't even legally question you as to how you spend it!"

"I think I must have heard you wrong, Mary. Are you telling me that any time my ex makes more money for himself, possibly by working overtime, improving his education, or taking on a better-paying job, I get more child support money without doing anything extra? I mean, if I marry someone, have his child, then divorce him, but he becomes financially successful in the future, does that mean that my income potential could be limitless simply because we had a child together, or do I have a few wires crossed here?"

"You've got it right, Molly. His success always translates into more money for you if you are getting support. I didn't create the system, I just administer it."

This suddenly struck me as being horrible. There is absolutely no incentive for any man going through divorce to work harder to make more money. The divorce system has made it impossible for these men to get ahead. I sure as hell wouldn't bust my butt if I were simply going to have to turn around and hand over my hard-earned paycheque to an ex who just sat there greedily waiting for more and more money with a smug look of 'entitlement' on her face!

"I haven't even told you the whole story yet, Molly," Mary continued. "There is another expense he has to pay you, along with, but separate from, the actual child support payment. It's what we call, 'extra-ordinary' expenses. This is money paid out for expenses not covered by the actual child support dollars, such as, but not limited to, childcare, summer camps, dental, medical, and sporting activities. These expenses are shared by both of you but are separate from child support dollars."

I shook my head in disbelief. With all the financial perks I was being given, it would be Christmas at my house every day. I knew that once my ex deducted taxes, child support, and all of those extra expenses from his paycheque, he would struggle to survive. Retirement for him would only be a dream. Once the children were older and education costs got added back in, he would be financially dead in the water. It was scary! I had the power in my hands to literally plunk him into the poorhouse at will. If I chose to be an angry or vindictive ex-wife, I could easily get my revenge on him; I could simply use the family laws already in place and force him into paying out money that I know he didn't have to give. I could leave him with next to nothing yet live quite comfortably myself.

I could even visualize the strategy available to take his money. If he refused to pay me for whatever extraordinary expenses I had dreamed up long after the divorce papers were signed, I could simply threaten him with court action. After all, with all the money I would already be getting from him, I'm sure he would be hard pressed to find the cash to even hire a lawyer. It would cost him more to fight me in court than to just roll over, play dead, and give me what I wanted. If he were dumb enough to fight me, I could just bleed him financially in court until he was ruined. I wouldn't need to be worried in the least. After all, his money would eventually run out, but my supply would be endless.

I wondered how many women out there actually thought this way. The temptation to be greedy was difficult to ignore. I only needed to give the "go ahead" command, then just sit back and watch the legal system devour my ex like a vicious dog. "It's not my fault you're ruined," I could say. "It's not my fault that you can't afford to buy anything for your children when they are with you. I didn't make the laws. The legal system is fair. They're just doing their job. I can't help it if you're angry!" It would be technically perfect: I give the orders, but the legal system inflicts the wounds. What a perfect vehicle for "legalized harassment." It was sheer genius. Still, I knew it was wrong.

"You can't squeeze blood from a stone," I finally said to Mary, embarrassed by the thoughts that I'd allowed to go through my head. "Where would he get the money to pay for all of this and still eat and pay his own bills?"

Mary's reply struck me as very cold. It lacked any sense of empathy for what any man must be feeling or going through emotionally during divorce. She simply said, "It's not your concern, Molly. He would have to either get a loan or borrow money from family or friends. He has to pay, no matter what his circumstances are. It's the law. Oh, and by the way, if you are worried about him not paying support, don't be. The family law legal system has created an effective watchdog to combat any of these deadbeat dads."

"Deadbeat dads?" I asked.

"You know, men who refuse to pay support or who miss even a single payment. We label them deadbeat dads. It helps to drum up community and media support for all the victimized mothers and the government-funded feminist groups. It's an amazing method of shaming men into stepping up to the plate and taking care of their own children. Actually, Molly, if you give me a second, I'll go to the Website. It's called the Family Responsibility Office, or the FRO. In fact, Molly, for our worst non-paying offenders, I can show you an area on our Website where we post 'wanted posters' with their pictures for the entire world to see. We include the last known place of residence and any personal information we have on file. These deadbeat dads can run, but they can't hide."

Mary clicked the mouse over and over, working her way through various computer screens to get to the FRO site. Even this early in my conversation with her, I was sensing that this was a legal system designed to punish men and that it was based on the assumption that all men are inherently irresponsible and can't be trusted to do what is right. With what I had been told thus far, the system of family law appeared to me, at least on the surface, to be biased against men's rights. I waited for Mary to finish on the computer.

Did the FRO ever take into account that some of these "wanted men" may actually be decent husbands and loving fathers who had every intention of paying but had possibly lost their jobs or fallen ill before having their pictures posted and their dignity destroyed? Did these men deserve to be treated on the same level by our judicial system as murderers and hardened criminals? What purpose would be served by humiliating these men in the eyes of their children, especially if their children had access to the Internet? It was too early in my meeting with Mary to pass a final verdict on this judicial process, but deep within my heart, I think I already knew that my patience and fiery Irish temper were going to be tested as the afternoon wore on.

CHAPTER THREE

Once Mary had finished, I walked behind her desk, leaned over her shoulder, and studied the information on the computer screen. She began to explain the Website to me. "If your ex-husband misses or is late on even one support payment, you can file your support order with the FRO, and they will make sure that you get paid whatever you deserve. The FRO, with support of the courts, has the authority to go in and garnish his wages, register a charge against his personal property, take money right from his bank account, suspend his driver's licence, report him to the credit bureau, and, if necessary, throw him in jail. It's quite an efficient system."

"So what you are telling me is that if a man doesn't pay his support, no matter what the circumstances are, you have the power to make his life hell, destroy his future, and dash any hope for recovery? Am I hearing you right?" I asked.

"It may seem harsh, Molly, but understand that this is all being done for the good of the children. By the way, do you want to see some of our wanted posters?"

"That's all right," I said coldly. "I've seen enough."

I could feel myself getting angry. I was tired of hearing phrases like "entitlement" and "for the good of the children." I had no use for a system that acted like "big brother" watching over my ex-husband's every move. We had already worked out an agreement together, as friends. I trusted him. I trusted his word. I wanted this legal system and all its rules and regulations to go away and stop making a simple and amicable separation complicated and unfair.

I was the one making the larger income. Surely, after all our years of marriage, we could work out something without court-imposed rules. We had always worked out any problems that had arisen during our marriage. Why did we now need the courts to interfere and attempt to solve problems that didn't even exist? This whole court thing was beginning to smell like a big cash-grab, just as my cousin had warned me.

Mary didn't know it yet, but I had no intention of accepting child support. I was determined to leave my ex with enough money to live, as well as to provide for our children when they were with him. If I didn't, how could he ever have the opportunity to be a parent to our kids? What good would be served by not leaving him enough money to feed our children, buy them necessities, or take them out for some fun? I wasn't a lawyer, but to me, this whole system seemed to lack a conscience. It was time that I got some things off my chest.

"Mary, I'm confused. Please explain how taking away a man's drivers licence, so that he can't get to work and might possibly lose his job, is in the best interest of the children? What if he is a truck or cab driver? What if he is in sales and has to drive all across the country to make a living? If you take away his ability to make an income, then of course he can't pay support. He automatically becomes one of your deadbeat dads! Is that really his fault or yours? Explain to me how draining his bank account and ruining his credit so he can't eat, get a loan or even a place to live is somehow going to be for the good of his children."

I could feel my Irish blood beginning to boil as I continued to fire up. "Can anyone please explain to me how ruining a man's life or forcing him to live a life on the streets is for the good of his children? How can a man with nothing left to his name be a father? These men have no chance of competing for the affections of their own children when they are up against ex-wives with pockets full of child and spousal support dollars. A child will gravitate to where the money is. Who can blame them? The individual who wields the money can buy the child's affections, create a fun Disneyland-type home environment, and be viewed by the child as the hero and stable parent–all because they can afford to cater to the child's every whim. Mary, these men are in a no-win situation. If this system is truly designed to help children, then let dads be dads. Children need the love of their fathers more than they need money. I loved my father with all my heart. What we lacked in material possessions, we made up twentyfold in love. I'll tell you one thing: We had each other, and those memories are more valuable to me now in adulthood than any stuff you could have bought me as a child. This system is cruel and heartless, if you ask me!"

My voice had become so hoarse from talking that I had to stop. I went back to my chair, sat down, and just stared out towards the door. I was fuming mad. "I'm sorry, Mary, if I seem angry, but this is just wrong. When I see an injustice, I just can't stay quiet. It's not in my nature."

Mary smiled weakly at me and said, "I know the system isn't perfect, but I'm just trying to do my job. I have to go over all of your rights with you, good or bad, so that you can make informed decisions."

"Mary, all I've seen so far is how family law protects women's rights! What about men's rights? How does this supposedly unbiased system look out for their needs? I bet there are a lot of good men out there, loving fathers, who get thrown to the curb, so to speak, because of these rules. They seem so inflexible! So black-and-white! So one-sided! It seems to me like none of the lawmakers left any room within the system for discussion of an individual's life circumstances before these life-altering legal decisions are made. A legal system has to have some sense of compassion built into it, don't you agree?"

I could tell by the disinterested look on Mary's face that I might as well have been talking to a wall. "We had better move on to the next topic, Molly. My next client will be here soon." I was beginning to think that she wished I'd gone somewhere else for my legal advice. "I need to talk to you about spousal support. The fact that you currently make more money than your ex means that he could come after you for support. The good news here is that as long as you keep the three children living with you, you're in the driver's seat. Family law views those children and their primary caregiver–that's you–as their number-one priority; therefore, if you ever find yourself out of work for any reason, don't worry. We would simply inform the court of your situation and ask that your ex begin making spousal support payments. After all, those children need food, clothing, and a roof over their heads. Someone has to pay, right? Better him than you."

"So, if I can't work or I lose my job, it's his responsibility to take care of me, simply because we got married? Have I got this right?"

"Spousal support is there to make sure that the standard of living that you and your children became accustomed to during the course of the marriage is kept constant even after the divorce is finalized. The time period for which spousal support payments are made is generally based on the number of years that you two were married. The unwritten rule of thumb that I've heard bantered around the courts is that if you were married for five, you pay for five, ten for ten, and if you were married for twenty-five, you pay for life! If, for example, the man is the support payer, then the actual payment amounts are based on his level of income. The more he makes, the more you get, which translates into an even better standard of living for you and the children. Remember, the courts are looking out for the best interests of you and the children."

I had to voice my opinion on this topic!

"What about the man's standard of living after divorce?" I asked. "Is that of no concern to the courts? Have you or your legal system ever stopped to think that I might actually care about his well-being? If my ex and I accept the fact that our 'collective' standard of living will be reduced because of divorce, then the children will have a consistent standard of living, whether they are with their mom or dad. If it's a level playing field, with all other things being equal, then the children should have no reason to favour being with one parent over the other."

Mary tried to interrupt me but I continued. "I'm already going to get child support. If my children are fed and taken care of, why wouldn't I go out and get another job? I've got two legs. You expect the man to work, so why shouldn't I? I can make my own damn money! If I'm fully capable of working, yet the system allows me to ride his back financially because we were married, then you're going to create a lot of 'kept' stay-at-home women. I'll tell you this much: If I was a man, I'd stay the hell away from marriage if that's the case."

I stopped for a moment. I just sat there and stared at Mary. I waited patiently for her rebuttal to my questions and concerns. I expected that her answer would be vague yet somehow politically correct. I knew that she wasn't going to have any explanation that would satisfy me. Her response was, however, worse than I had expected. She stared back at me and shrugged her shoulders, as if saying, "What do you expect me to do about the system?"

I looked back at her in bewilderment. I wondered if anyone in the legal system ever questioned the rules they were expected to enforce. Didn't anyone ever wonder if the laws were even fair or logical or made sense? I bet if a few of our well-paid politicians, lawyers, or judges came out on the wrong end of a divorce battle, we'd all see the changes fly.

The more I thought about it, this whole spousal support thing seemed like nothing more than a good way for the government to avoid paying out taxpayer money to women who either weren't working or could possibly become a financial burden on the system in the future. I could even hear the government's slogan in my head: "You married them, you take care of them." I had to give the government an "A" for ingenuity. They had, in essence, turned men into a personal and bottomless type of welfare system for women.

"Answer me this, Mary, before we leave the topic of spousal and child support, since it just occurred to me. Let's say that after getting divorced, I start dating again. After six months of me dating some new man in my life, he moves in with me and my kids. He then gets close to my children and does a lot of fatherly type things with them. Unfortunately, we never get married because the relationship goes sour. He moves out and on with his life. I wouldn't do this, but could I legally go after him for child support, as well as the children's biological father?"

Mary was quick to answer."If this new man can be shown to have taken on a parental role in the life of your children, then in the eyes of the court, the answer is yes."

"You've got to be kidding," I said. "Think about it. That's financial double dipping. Two support payments for one child. What a concept! Imagine if a woman had no conscience and just wanted to make money. She could have quite a cozy life, just by creating a revolving-door dating system."

"A revolving what?" Mary asked, not quite sure of what I was getting at.

"Let me explain to you how my idea would work," I said. "First, you draw the man in and stroke his ego a bit, pretend you're interested in him. Smile at him a lot and give him good sex for at least six months to a year. Make sure he moves in–that's the key. Next, give him plenty of time to become a father figure in your child's life, and then, wham! Make up some reason to end the relationship, show him the exit door, permanently, and then call your friendly neighbourhood lawyer. Off to court you go. Scoop up the child support money, and then on to the next man. It would be so easy."

"Molly, we don't like to think of it like that. As a legal system, we would hope that women have more ethics than that."

"So do I, Mary, but in theory, could this happen?"

Just as she was about to answer, Mary developed a tickle in her throat and began to cough but nodded her head in agreement as she excused herself to get a drink of water.

CHAPTER FOUR

Sitting there, I started to fantasize just how great it would be to have all that free money. I kept trying to shake off the greed that was welling up deep inside of me. I knew that I had promised not to hurt my now ex-husband, but it was so hard. I even went so far as to ponder what my life would be like if I were to marry and then divorce a rich second husband. I'd be living on easy street. Hell, I wouldn't even have to work. From child support alone, I'd be set. Never mind the spousal support the courts would throw in for good measure.

Then another scenario popped into my head. This one was even better. I am twenty, sexy, and curvy again. In this scenario, I imagine myself wanting a baby, but without all the baggage a relationship could create. I see myself using my feminine ways to get pregnant without my partner even knowing. Then, I end this relationship of convenience and force him to pay me child support. Hell, I'd have the law on my side. I'd have my baby, a constant stream of money, and no man. *Keep it clean and simple,* I thought. Like the scenario before, this man would definitely be rich.

"That is quite enough of that way of thinking, young lady," I said to myself. I chuckled under my breath and said, "Don't worry, God. I'm not that kind of person. You know me. I'll always listen to the angel on my shoulder, and not the devil."

Just then, Mary walked back into the room, waving her finger in the air in my direction. "As I was getting my water, I realized that I'd forgotten to tell you one last thing about child and spousal support before we go on."

That's it, I thought to myself, *I've had enough*. I interrupted Mary just as she was about to continue. "This meeting is over. I can't do this. I'm sure some women love listening to what you've got to say. They probably wring their hands and drool over all the money they can have at the expense of another human being, but not me. I have to live with myself. I like who I see in the mirror each morning, and I'm going to keep it that way.

"Tell me something, Mary. When does the financial bloodletting ever end for these men? Why not just suck out their wallets with a vacuum cleaner? It would be faster and probably just as effective. By the way, I'm going to stick to the original plan that my ex and I put together....you know, the one still sitting in my purse. And as far as child support goes, I don't want it! I've got a very good job, and between the two of us, the children will be well taken care of."

Mary began to talk as I rummaged through my purse looking for the agreement I had brought in. "Molly, please! Stop and listen! It is highly unlikely that any judge will ever sign off on your divorce unless you accept child support. You really have little choice in this matter."

Oh, I stopped all right! You could have heard a pin drop after her words came out. I slowly lifted my head and met her gaze head-on. I squeezed my purse straps tightly between my fingers and chose my next comments carefully and methodically so as to keep my anger and frustration in check.

"Mary, we all have what I call pivotal moments in our life. This conversation was one of mine. When I married my husband, our vows were all about love and honor, not greed, gluttony, revenge, or entitlement. Talking with you today has only solidified for me what I already suspected–that our lawmakers have created a system in which the pendulum of power has swung way too far in favor of women. In my opinion, divorce is going to destroy the very institution of marriage. Why would a man ever get married when he has everything to lose? It is the woman who has everything to gain. For most men, marriage is a crapshoot. For most women, marriage is, at its worst, a financial windfall. In my eyes, this is a predatory legal system, Mary, where a woman with no ethics or morals can make a profitable business for herself by marrying and divorcing rich men."

By this time, I had put my coat on and was about to leave, but not until I had finished speaking my mind. "Mary, this system pits people against each other, creating unnecessary conflict. Take my case, for example. I came to you with a well-thought-out divorce plan, yet the legal system has decided for me that I can't get divorced unless I lie to you and tell you that I want child support when, in fact, I don't. Look at the position I have just put my ex in. He has to sign the divorce papers, trusting that I'm still good for my word. I have taken control of his financial future. I promised him that I never would. When will the government take its nose out of people's affairs and respect their wishes? Without even trying, the legal system has created conflict within our divorce process. If my ex and I had not been rational, trusting people, this issue could have exploded into a much larger problem. And as you and I both know, the only winner if that happens is the lawyer."

With much animosity, I then took the pen from Mary's outstretched hand and signed the papers. Once I looked down and actually saw my signature on those legal documents, I felt like I had sold out both my values and my husband. I had just been sucked in by the very system to which I had vowed never to succumb.

CHAPTER FIVE

I had to keep wiping the tears from my eyes as I drove home. But these tears weren't for me; they were for all those men who were being taken advantage of by a system that wiped the floor with them. I was sad for the men who were treated like expendable commodities, except for their wallets.

I decided to pull my car over and phone my ex on my cell phone. I was too angry to drive. When he answered, I blurted out, "Is this legal system as bad as I think it is? Tell me it isn't, please!" I began to tell him about my meeting with Mary and how we most likely couldn't get divorced if I didn't accept child support. I told him about the financial buffet laid out at my feet. I told him everything. As the words tumbled off my lips, all I could hear in my head, over and over, was "This is so wrong!"

After listening to me, all he could say was "I'm not surprised." It took him a few seconds to gather his thoughts, and then he began to elaborate. He told me that a number of men in the small crew that he worked with were divorced and he had heard the horror stories from many of them. They jokingly called the newly separated men 'newbies' to distinguish them from the battle-weary veterans who had already lost virtually everything.

He said that the script never changes very much. The soon-to-be-divorced man is first displaced from his home. Then he signs over his house and a large chunk of his pension and investments to his ex-wife. Her standard of living is usually left unscathed or even gets better while he is left to live a meagre existence in some dingy little apartment. The ex-husband starts paying spousal and child support, left to survive paycheque to paycheque, with little hope of financial recovery or retirement.

To make matters worse, he is usually emotional, so he hires an expensive lawyer to fight for his right to equal parenting for his children, though this fight all too often ends with his own financial ruin because of the enormous legal cost. He then settles for the standard court access schedule of every other weekend and Wednesday night. Once the ex-wife learns that he is broke, she will either go away peacefully now that there is nothing left to gain or will take him back to court until he is left with less than nothing. If the ex is really out for blood, she will either turn the kids against him or force him back to court with a barrage of false accusations until he breaks emotionally and gives her sole custody. If this is the case, he usually fades into obscurity from the lives of his children and his ex–unless, of course, she needs more money.

"I'll tell you, Molly, we have divorced men working here that fit into each of those scenarios. The one constant among them is that they are all very angry. They are angry with the lawyers who let them down and with the women they once loved who turned against them. They all tell me that they had no voice in court. They were always perceived as guilty until proven innocent. It's so sad, Molly. Most of these men are working day in and day out to simply pay for their ex-wife's lifestyle. In the end, there is little left for them.

"A few of these guys have tried getting involved in a new relationship after being divorced, but once the new girlfriend learns that her income could eventually be added to his in order to calculate higher spousal and child support payments for his ex-wife, she runs for the hills. You can't blame these women. Why would they want to part with their hard-earned dollars only to give it to ex-wives they don't even know?

"So, there you have it, Molly–divorce in a nutshell. Or at least what I see every day. The question I keep asking myself is, "If the system is fair, then why are most divorced men left financially ruined?"

He was asking me questions for which I had no answers. To me, his questions sounded more like cries of frustration or desperation, for both his struggling co-workers and a legal system that, as we both saw, chews up and spits out husbands and good fathers every day.

Before hanging up, he left me with some words that were insightful yet sad. He told me that even though these men he talked about were broken, they were not defeated. Divorced men are like a family, and, just as family members help each other out in times of crisis, these men help each other deal with the trauma, stress, and depression that often accompany divorce. They do their best to support each other. In the end, few of these men ever end up having any meaningful contact with their children, and they are too untrusting of women to ever date again, but they band together, never believing that change is impossible or that life won't get better.

"All of them tell me that they carry on because of the love they have for their children. These men generally don't shed tears in public, but there is an unspoken bond between them. They always have each other's shoulders to lean on if the struggle becomes too great for any one man to bear."

He closed our conversation with a touching statement. "Thank you, Molly, for respecting me as both a father and a husband. You have the kindest heart of anyone I have ever met. We will always be friends, and I doubt I will ever meet anyone else with as gentle a spirit as you."

I sat at the side of the road, awestruck by how peacefully and respectfully a marriage could end if both partners simply worked things out. The formula is simple; Communication is the key. I won't hurt him, he won't hurt me, and we will both put the best interests of our children first. Why don't people get it? God must be so sad right now. This isn't how he intended us to act towards one another, fighting, arguing, and destroying each other's lives.

I slipped my cell phone back into its case before starting the car. It was one-thirty, and the children wouldn't be getting home from school until four o'clock, so I decided to stop for a coffee and sandwich before heading home. It had been a long day, and I needed to escape all of this toxicity for a few moments. I wanted to greet my children with a clear head, and, besides, I hadn't eaten anything all day.

I stood in line at the coffee shop, thinking about the events of the past few hours. I gave the young lady at the cash register my order, waited, and slowly let out a huge sigh. It felt good to be out of that paralegal office. I couldn't fathom how any man or woman could swim in that sea of legal garbage for any length of time without becoming physically ill.

The lady at the cash register called out my order number. It startled me out of my distant state and caused me to drop my open purse and all its contents on the floor. Noticing my predicament, several people began retrieving my things and started stuffing everything from lipstick to old gum wrappers into my hands. I graciously thanked everyone, paid for my meal, and quickly turned for the deepest, darkest corner of the restaurant where I could hide away and eat my meal in peace. I found a quiet little table in the corner and had just set my tray down when a voice called out from behind me. "Miss, excuse me, you also dropped this." I turned around and was handed a small piece of paper by a young man.

"Thank you" I said as I took the object. I stuffed it into my coat pocket and settled in for my meal.

I sat with my back to the interior of the restaurant and began to eat my sandwich. My stomach was still feeling nauseous, but the food tasted good. As I took the first sip of my coffee, I reached my hand into my coat pocket and fished around for that little piece of paper. I finally found it wedged underneath a pile of keys. I placed it on my lunch tray and began unfolding its tightly creased edges, yet it still looked like nothing more than a white piece of paper to me–until I turned it over.

It was a picture of my best friend, Bill. He had died, much too young, in a car crash, right in the midst of a horrific divorce. I had watched him go through it, but I had not understood at the time what to say or, really, how to help him. I had felt empathy for him and his plight, but at the time, I had been happily married and unable to connect to his pain. I wondered why God was showing me his picture at this moment. I felt that deep connection to Bill resurfacing as I looked down at those piercing blue eyes.

"No one can understand the depth of pain you're in until they live through it themselves, can they, Bill?" I mumbled. I couldn't stop staring at his picture. It had been years since I'd last seen it.

I lifted his picture closer to my face to examine every feature in detail. My other hand continued to methodically stir my coffee, not even realizing that it had long since gone cold. In the corner of that quiet little coffee shop, time suddenly stood still, and my thoughts once again carried me back to the day we had met.

I first met Bill when I was in my early twenties and about to graduate from nursing college. My sister introduced us to each other at a barbeque at her house. Anne warned me that Bill was a private person who didn't generally let people get close to him so not to get upset if he didn't talk to me much. To the contrary, we hit it off immediately as we both had the same crazy sense of humour. Our personalities meshed together beautifully, and because of that, we quickly developed a deep and lasting friendship.

As I got to know him better, I realized that Bill also took pleasure in the simple things in life and didn't take himself too seriously. Bill loved to play horseshoes; it was his passion. I spent many a lazy Sunday afternoon attempting to learn the fine art of tossing shoes while enjoying a cold beer, talking about life under his big oak tree, or just touring around in his trusty Ford Mustang with no real destination in mind. Everyone thought that we would eventually get married because we spent most of our spare time together, but in reality, our relationship was more like that of big brother and little sister. I felt safe and cared for when I was with him. Our relationship never went past that of friendship.

Life eventually got in the way, and we fell out of touch. I heard through a mutual friend that Bill had met and started dating a lady named Barbara. I was overjoyed when Bill phoned me one day, out of the blue, and invited me to his parents' house for a barbeque the following Saturday. He said it would be a good chance for us to reminisce about old times, and he was excited for me to meet Barbara.

I wasn't prepared for the frosty reception that Barbara had in store for me. Once at the barbeque, I barely had time to get out of my car before Bill ran up to me, gave me a big bear hug, told me how much he missed me, and began telling everyone within earshot, including Barbara, about all the fun things we had done together when we were younger. It was hot that August afternoon, but I had chills running down my spine from Barbara glaring at me the whole day. I knew as I left that night that I would no longer be welcome in Bill's life as long as Barbara was in the picture.

Over the next year, I phoned Bill a few times and left messages, but he never returned my calls. I had about given up on our friendship when, out of the blue, I received an unexpected call from him. He sounded panicky, asking me in a whispered voice if I would meet him the following Wednesday night at his house around seven. "I can't talk right now," he said, "but I'll explain everything to you when you get here." As soon as I said I'd be there, he hung up.

When I walked through his front door the following Wednesday, Bill immediately started apologizing. "I'm sorry I didn't return your calls, Molly, but Barbara can't stand you. I don't know why. I think she's either jealous of you, our relationship, or both. Either way, she had forbidden me from talking to you. If she even got wind of the fact that you're here tonight, I'd be in big trouble."

I couldn't believe what I was hearing. The old Bill I had known would never allow himself to be controlled by anyone. "Bill," I said, "you're not married to her. Why don't you just end the relationship and move on?" A long silence followed. Bill just sat on the couch with his head down, saying nothing. "What's going on? What aren't you telling me?"

There was another long pause, and then Bill erupted. "I can't leave, Molly. I got her pregnant!"

"You did what?" I said in disbelief. I didn't know what to do, so I sat down next to him on the couch and held his hand for support. He then continued.

"When we started dating, she was wonderful. I felt cared for, and it all seemed too good to be true. I guess it was, because once she got pregnant, everything changed. She changed. This angry side of her emerged, sometimes to the point of real violence. And controlling! She needed to know my every move, my every whereabouts, and she became extremely jealous of me having any female friends, especially you. Ever since that barbeque, I can't mention your name without a fight erupting."

Bill went on to tell me that he had first met Barbara while she was working part-time as a waitress at a local restaurant he frequented. Over time, a friendship had developed and he had eventually asked her out on a date. She had brought a daughter from a previous relationship into the mix, but Bill hadn't cared. He told me that as the relationship had progressed, he'd begun to love her daughter as if she were his own.

"Do you love Barbara?" I asked him point-blank.

"Does that really matter? I'm going to marry her. It's the right thing to do. I got her pregnant. My father always raised me to do the honourable thing."

"Let me ask you a couple of questions," I said. "When Barbara got pregnant, were you using birth control?"

"She told me that she was on the pill. Why?"

"I was just wondering. Now tell me, was she interested in dating you before or after she found out that you have a successful business? Be honest, because I know you'd tell her."

"I'd say it was after. Why do you care? What are you getting at?" I could tell by the naive look on his face that it wasn't going to be easy to get the light bulb to go off in his head.

"I've got to go," I said, "but I'm going to leave you with one last thing to think about. Ask yourself this question before your wedding day: Would she still be willing to marry you even if you were poor? If you answer yes, that's great. But if you hesitate for even a second or have to think about your answer, then I suggest that you reconsider your decision to get married. Once you put that ring on her finger, whether you love her or hate her, stay in the relationship or leave, it won't matter anymore. Either way, you've just given her free reign to take everything you've worked your whole life for. Think about what I've said, that's all I'm asking."

My words unnerved Bill, but he stuck by his decision to marry Barbara. Our friendship once again faded into obscurity until years later, when I received a frantic early-morning phone call from his sister, Rebecca.

"He's really angry, Molly," she began. "I know you haven't talked to him for years, but you're the only person he'll listen to. He's going through a divorce from hell, and he needs your help. I'm worried that he's going to crack under the pressure and do something stupid like take his own life. He told me what you said that day, warning him about getting married. He should have listened to you. You were right."

I cancelled work for the day, got Bill's new address from his sister, and drove out to the apartment where he was living. When I pulled up to the building, my heart sank. From the outside, it looked old and run down. Inside, the paint on the lobby walls was peeling, and the inside of the elevator smelled like stale beer. It was difficult to read the apartment numbers because the hall lighting was poor. I made my way down the hall to apartment 507 and knocked on the door. After a few clicks of the door locks, the door swung open and I was once again standing face-to-face with my old friend.

He looked shocked to see me. I could tell from his reaction that his sister hadn't warned him that I was coming. Bill had aged a lot since I'd last seen him. His hair was beginning to gray, and his face looked drawn and pale. He had lost far too much weight, and his boyish grin was gone. It had been replaced with a flat, expressionless stare. As I opened my arms to hug him, he broke down and embraced me.

"I was so stupid to let our friendship end the way it did, Molly. I won't ever let that happen again. You were right all along about Barbara. She's trying to take everything from me, including my children. I'm so scared she'll win. I miss my kids so much!"

I took Bill by the shoulders and made him look me straight in the eyes. "Bill, I'm not going to abandon you," I said. "We're going to get you through this, but you've got to be strong."

We sat at his kitchen table, where he began to open up to me. He told me about Barbara's abuse of their children, her random bouts of depression and anger, her reluctance to seek treatment, and the lack of intimacy within their relationship.

We talked more that day than we had in years. Bill stayed true to his word, never again letting anyone interfere in our relationship. He was unable to stop Barbara from interfering in his relationship with his children, however. He said that she would use the children as pawns to get what she wanted. If he didn't play the game by her rules, she would refuse him access to the children. In fact, the Christmas before he died, Bill was forced to call the police and show them a copy of the court order outlining his access schedule for visitation before Barbara would release the children to him. Even after breaking a court order, Barbara was never held accountable for her actions. Bill had no money to take her back to court, and she knew it. In Bill's eyes, his support payments were supporting her ability to function "outside the law" without fear of any legal action against her. She had begun documenting his every move, hoping to stress him to the point that he would "lose it" emotionally in front of the children so she could prove in court that he was an unfit father. The stress in Bill's life was relentless.

The last time we talked was two weeks before Bill's death. We talked about life, marriage, and even God. I listened intently to his every word. He was more philosophical than angry that day, which made me more interested in hearing what he had to say.

"Relationships need the test of time, Molly, because people change. A good relationship is like a fine wine. It takes years to develop, but the end result in both cases is sweet and worth the wait. Can you honestly look at your partner and say that you'll be together until you die? I don't think so. The best thing you can do for yourself is never get married. If you get married, make sure that you marry your best friend, because a marriage may be short lived, but a woman's wrath can last a lifetime. Just look at what I've gone through.

"And why do you have to sign documents and say vows in order to justify your love for one another? To me, a marriage certificate is simply an insurance policy you sign, issued by the government to ensure that you are financially responsible for your spouse until you die. If you and your partner simply want to express your vows of love and commitment to one another in front of God, you don't need a church. Just go into your back-yard and say them in private. God is everywhere.

"You don't stay with someone because of a ring on their finger or because of some vow. You stay in a relationship because you love each other, and that's the bottom line. If you both believe that your love will last forever, then why do you need a legal contract of marriage? Can love be contracted? You can't contract something that is natural. Love is a feeling."

Bill's words really touched me that day. Before I left his apartment that afternoon, Bill gave me one of his usual bear hugs. "Thanks for listening to me today. You're the best. I love you. Now get out of here before I get emotional."

"I love you too," I called back as I walked down the hall toward the elevator.

I could never have imagined that, as I heard his apartment door close behind me, I would never talk to him again. The next contact I would have with Bill would be at his funeral.

CHAPTER SIX

It was a Sunday afternoon, and I was in the middle of some house cleaning when the phone rang. I rushed to the bedroom to answer it, hoping it was Bill. We were planning to get together later that day or possibly on the following Monday. When I picked up the receiver, all I could hear was Bill's oldest daughter, Amy, crying uncontrollably on the other end of the line.

"Are you OK?" I demanded. Since his divorce, Bill's children had informed him several times that their mother had abused them. Bill had notified the Children's Aid Society (CAS) of his concerns.

"Have you talked to your dad?" I asked, my voice now full of concern. Still, only tears and sobs kept coming from the other end. "Talk to me, Amy! Please! Say something! What's wrong?" By this time, I was getting so upset that I had started yelling into the receiver. "Amy, stay where you are! I'll call your dad and get him to come and pick you and your sisters up right away!" Before she could even respond, I had already hung up the phone.

Oh, my God, here we go again, I thought as I punched Bill's number into my phone. I prayed that this time the courts would finally listen to him and take the allegations of child abuse seriously. Maybe now he could get his children back, hopefully for good. I was filled with empathy for Bill, who had already endured a four-year struggle with Family Court and his ex-wife and her lawyer, with no end in sight. There was nothing I could do other than continue giving him my moral support.

As I continued to dial Bill's number with no response, I couldn't stop thinking of just how much I cared for these children. Hearing Amy's voice full of fear and anxiety had brought back a flood of memories surrounding Bill and his children. I remembered the time I had talked with Bill late one Sunday evening after he had returned home from dropping off his kids at his ex-wife's house. He had described, in painful detail, how his youngest daughter had clung to him like a koala bear cub hugging its mother as he had tried to put her into the car seat for the long drive back to her mother's. She had cried out, "I don't want to go! Please! I want to stay with you!" while gasping through her tears. Her muffled voice had resonated deep into his chest as she had struggled to get free of the car-seat restraints. Bill had been so angry that a court order was taking precedence over a father's ability to protect his children.

There were other occasions when Bill had described bruises he had found on his children. They had begged him to help them, as they were becoming increasingly frightened by their mother's violent temper. They were afraid to talk about him in their mother's presence because they did not want to incite her temper. He had told his lawyer that his ex-wife had an anger-management problem and that he was worried about the possibility of her abusing the children. His lawyer had done nothing with this information, and all of the concerns Bill had brought up in court concerning his ex-wife had become bitter reality.

The family laws were instrumental in helping to imprison Bill's children, against their wills, with an abusive mother in an unsafe environment. Bill had surmised that this biased legal decision had been carried out based on the premise that men and women are only considered equally capable co-parents by the courts up until the time of divorce. After that, women somehow magically take on a superior ability to raise young children. The men, who have been capable fathers to their children until the divorce, become nothing more than weekend visitors or casual playmates at that time.

"But they want to live with me!" Bill would yell out, his hands wiping away tears of frustration. I felt incredibly sorry for him during those moments of inner turmoil and emotional darkness. It was important that I let him vent his anger at a legal system that left him feeling helpless.

"Why won't the courts let my children have a voice?" he would ask. "Why won't the courts just leave me alone? Please! Just let me be a father and love my children!"

I couldn't even begin to comprehend the pain that Bill was carrying around within his heart. He once told me that the divorce laws were ironclad when it came to the issue of children and access. He knew that, because his ex had sole custody of their children, he could never step on her property or enter her house without consent, even if he believed his children's lives were in danger, because he could be charged and thrown in jail. I remember him saying that he believed his children would have to be bloodied, dead, or both before the courts would take them away from their mother.

Bill had fought vigorously for sole custody of his children, even after his divorce was finalized. He had spent thousands of dollars on legal bills, but had gotten nowhere. The large support payments he paid out each month began to quickly drain his once-healthy bank account. In contrast, this same money had only served to strengthen his ex-wife's financial war chest, supplying her lawyer with a steady stream of financial ammunition with which to continue the attacks against him in court. Bill had known that even if he were eventually forced into bankruptcy while fighting for his children, he would still have to make support payments. He was stuck trying to fight a system that could never let him win.

Even Bill's pleas to the Children's Aid Society concerning allegations of child abuse had fallen on deaf ears. One evening, he had gone, sat, and talked to representatives from the CAS. During that meeting, they had taken notes and been sympathetic, but in the end, his concerns had been given nothing more than lip service. They had gone over to his ex's house and told her who had filed the accusations. Then they'd asked her if Bill's allegations were in fact true. When she had emphatically denied any wrongdoing, the case had been promptly closed and filed away.

Unfortunately for Bill, the meeting with Children's Aid had served only to intensify his ex-wife's anger. To make matters worse, Bill was then racked with guilt. He was worried that his children would suffer even more abuse after being brave enough to open up to him. He feared that his ex-wife would view the children's actions as some type of betrayal against her. She intensified the focus of her anger towards Bill, using her lawyer as the vehicle to create any reason to repeatedly take him back to court and further reduce his access to the children.

He was afraid to go home at night because he never knew what new legal demand would be waiting for him in his mailbox. Bill was definitely in a Catch-22; he didn't have any money to fight his ex-wife in court, yet if he didn't defend himself against all the lies being hurled at him, the court would most likely find him guilty in his absence. He commented that he felt like his ex-wife, her lawyer, and the whole legal system were repeatedly harassing him.

Bill was always a very proud man. Up until this point in his life, I'd always complimented him on his positive attitude. He could see a silver lining in any situation, but this time was different. Divorce had robbed him of his children, and all he had ever wanted was time with his kids and to keep them safe.

William Shakespeare once said, "The eyes are the mirror to the soul." If that was the case, then Bill's soul was dying. I could see it in his eyes. I had just prayed that he would never give up his will to live. His children needed a father, regardless of what the courts or the lawyers would lead one to believe.

I think that his ex-wife believed that Bill needed to be punished for attempting to exert his influence over the upbringing of his own children. I believed that she viewed her sole custody over the children as an autonomous type of self-rule in which she was the alpha leader, or top dog, and that her parenting style was not to be challenged by anyone–especially Bill!

All these thoughts of Bill's children made me even more resigned to track him down. After receiving no response to repeated calls, I was beginning to get anxious. I decided to call his mother to see if she knew where he was. When Bill's mom, Karen, answered the phone, I started talking a mile a minute, explaining how Amy was in trouble and that Bill had to get her out of that house for good, no matter what the cost!

I stopped to catch my breath for a moment and give Karen a chance to jump in on the conversation. She was no stranger to the concerns her son had for the children, so I was surprised when she didn't say anything. I waited, yet there was nothing but extended silence.

Finally, she began to speak in a sombre, muted voice, her words broken by sobs. "Oh Molly," she said, "You were the one person we hadn't wanted to call. We know how close you and Bill were."

"What do you mean *were*?" I demanded. I braced myself for the worst. With the phone clutched tightly to my ear and my eyes closed, I began to pray under my breath as she broke the news to me.

"Bill was killed in a car crash Molly, just a few hours ago. His car was found flipped over in the ditch on a county road. He wasn't wearing his seat-belt."

I could sense the anger in Karen's words as she spoke. She'd lectured her son many times on the importance of wearing a seat-belt. In the past, he'd been able to pacify her fears by giving her a big hug and telling her to stop worrying. This time, there would be no pacifying her. "Molly, the police told us that his body ejected from the car on impact. He was pronounced dead at the scene. He didn't deserve to die that way!"

I tried to console Karen, but nothing would come out. I couldn't speak. I couldn't do anything. My world went dark. The next sound I heard was my own body hitting the bedroom floor as my legs buckled like broken twigs. I lay there, emotionally paralysed, for hours, unable to even lift my face from the floor. Every so often, I would hear wails of anguish permeate the room, sounds like a mother would make upon learning of the death of her child, yet somehow, I had become so detached from both my body and feelings that I didn't recognize that these guttural expulsions of indescribable pain were actually coming from me. My rational mind could not accept Bill's death. Death was not part of the equation of our friendship. "Buddies and soul mates to the end" we'd always said to each other. In that moment, I knew that death had cheated me out of my best friend, but worse, it had cheated the world out of an amazing human being.

The next day, I made my way out to the ditch where Bill had died. The car had been removed and taken to the wreckers, but the smell of gasoline still pierced the morning air. As I walked in amongst the flattened grass that marked the final resting place of Bill's car, I came across our last horseshoe game scores printed in pencil on a piece of paper lying next to a cluster of beautiful white daisies. (I had brought my three girls out to play horseshoes with Bill and his kids only a week earlier.) A few feet away, in the deepest part of the ditch, sat Bill's favourite sunglasses, splattered with droplets of blood. Next to them was our favourite Bryan Adams CD.

I wandered back and forth along the ditch, like a tiger pacing in its cage, searching for any memento of Bill's life. Each time I came across another memory of him, I would pick it up, gently clean it off, and place it lovingly in one of my coat pockets. Bill's car must have rolled once or twice before coming to rest, because I found his personal belongings scattered well away from the crash site.

Once I was satisfied that I had recovered everything I possibly could, I made my way back to the top of the ditch. I wanted to take one last moment to take in this final scene before heading back to my car. It all seemed surreal to me. Standing there, looking down that quiet county road, all I could hear was the sound of birds happily chirping in the treetops as if nothing had happened here. But something had happened. Three young children had just lost their father.

I prayed for Bill. I prayed that in death, he would finally find peace. Unfortunately for him, even death didn't mark the end of his abuse by the legal system–just the beginning of a new chapter. A new storm was brewing that would attack his family to its breaking point, and the knife was being sharpened even before his body was buried.

CHAPTER SEVEN

The cemetery was overflowing with family and friends on the day of Bill's funeral. Nearly everyone in his close-knit community came out to pay their last respects. He'd been self-employed, starting up a successful electrical business in his hometown by the age of twenty-four. Because of his honesty and dedication to precision, he had always been inundated with work. Whether it was rewiring a small bathroom or servicing a large commercial building, Bill had treated all of his customers with the same respect. They were not just his neighbours; they were his friends.

The entire community had rallied around Bill at the time of his divorce. In a small town, everyone talks, and everyone knows your business. His situation regarding his kids was no secret to his many friends. They could see the devastation on his face, the sadness in his eyes, and the defeat in his posture. Since his divorce, Bill had spent so much time in court battling his ex-wife for custody of his children that he had missed out on a lot of work due to his lack of availability. As the legal bills mounted and the support payments poured out, his once-profitable business had begun to slip toward financial ruin.

Bill's ex-wife and children were mong the many mourners gathered at the cemetery that day. It would've been hard to miss his ex in the crowd. Looking at her, I was struck by how impeccably dressed she was. She was decked out for the occasion in designer clothing from top to bottom. I remember that at the end of Bill's life, between paying support payments and legal bills, he often hadn't had enough money to cover his own most basic needs. Frozen dinners had become a regular staple of his daily diet, and a big splurge for him would have been buying a new pair of jeans. His small rented apartment was furnished with odds and ends he had inherited from friends or purchased in the local Goodwill store. The irony was that as Bill was rummaging through bargain bins, his ex and children were living in a beautiful fully furnished home that he had helped pay for through years of hard work.

Barbara had made sure that Bill was accountable for every penny his business earned by having her accountant and lawyer go through his financial records yearly. She had him under a financial microscope from which there was no escape, three hundred and sixty-five days of the year.

Bill had always been the epitome of generosity during their marriage. He had always put the needs of the family before his own, so there were no reasons for Barbara to police his finances after the marriage ended. Bill had never had a problem with paying support for his children, so it was hard to watch his last penny go towards designer clothing for his ex-wife, under the pretence that this money was being used for the good of the children.

As the minister spoke of Bill's life and quoted scripture from the Bible, his children stood solemn and tearful next to their father's casket. They each took a turn kissing the edge of the casket and laying a single white rose on top before it was slowly lowered into the ground. I could only imagine what they were feeling and thinking at that moment. They were too young to fully understand the finality of death, but they knew, as I did, that their father and protector was gone.

What I didn't know at the time was that as Barbara stood there in the cemetery, her lawyer was working feverishly behind the scenes. At her request, her lawyer was busy creating a strategic legal battle plan with which to steal the import-export business that Bill's parents had started year's earlier right out from under their feet.

Bill's father, Dave, was a very sweet man. When Bill and Barbara had first married, Bill's father had expressed his desire to someday turn the family business over to his only son. In that way, the business would carry on long after he had retired. Bill had been excited by this prospect.

It sickened me to learn that only days after Bill's funeral, the legal attack on his parent's business was launched. Just as Bill had been under a constant legal barrage during the end of his life; his parents were the new targets after his death. Barbara's divorce lawyer demanded to see every financial document, every transaction, and every piece of paper associated with the running of the business. The harassing of innocent human lives by the legal system had now taken an ugly turn. Bills parent's, who had had nothing to do with the divorce, were forced to hire their own lawyer to defend the existence of their own business.

According to Bill, Barbara had made little effort and had shown minimal interest in getting to know his parents when they were dating. Still, she had been welcomed into the family like a daughter, with unconditional love and acceptance. Now this same woman was trying to prove, using any legal avenue open to her, that Bill's father must have at some point, without her knowledge, signed the business over to his son. Her focus was now on taking over financial control of her in-laws' business with no regard as to whom she would hurt. In my opinion, the saddest thing is that this was ever allowed to happen.

In a letter to Bill's father from her lawyer, Barbara attempted to rationalize her motive for wanting to seize their assets—nothing personal, just business. She claimed that it was her duty to provide for her children's future and that she was simply laying claim to what was rightfully theirs. This was over and above being the sole beneficiary of a large life insurance policy that Bill had been forced to take out on his life by the family court at the time of his divorce. The last sentence of the letter said it all: "It's for the good of the children." Luckily, Bill's father had not yet signed the business over to anyone, so the plan fell apart.

Because of all this "legalized harassment," much of Bill's parents' savings ended up being consumed by legal bills. This couple had been forced into a legal battle they hadn't gone looking for. Why? Because of our legal system! It allows women to seek their supposed rightful entitlement with a vengeance and without fear of any legal repercussions from the party being attacked. In this case, it was an unfair battle on two fronts. First, Bill's parents were constantly put on the defensive, being forced to prove their innocence. Second, they had no time to catch their breath and grieve the loss of their only son.

So, who is policing the judges and the lawyers? Are there no rules of conduct as to what is just legal practice when it comes to the litigation of a divorce? In this case, Barbara and her lawyer followed their own sense of morality in their conduct, rather than a court-imposed one. They alone decided just how far they were willing to badger and harass this couple, pushing the envelope to its limit, solely for the attainment of money.

The legal attack left Dave and Karen distrustful of people. They'd watched their son's life fall to pieces after being divorced from Barbara. They'd felt his pain as he struggled for years to gain custody of his children and free them from the grip of an abusive mother, yet through all this turmoil, Bill's parents had always had to be on their best behaviour around Barbara, as she'd made it clear to them that if they stepped out of line, they could forget seeing their grandchildren again. This was not what they had bargained for when their son had fallen in love and gotten married.

If Bill were still here, I bet he'd say without question that his greatest downfall in life was quite simple. He had uttered those two fateful words that destroy men and empower women: "I do."

A restaurant attendant suddenly startled me out of my dreamlike state. "Are you finished? Would you like me to clear your table?"

At first I wasn't quite sure where I was. I tried to get my bearings. Then I glanced down at my watch. I couldn't believe it. I'd been lost deep in thought, thinking about Bill, for the last thirty minutes. I felt embarrassed at being caught daydreaming. I told the attendant to go ahead while I busied myself, by packing up my belonging. I looked at Bill's picture one last time before putting it in my purse, and heading for the exit. I loved Bill, but there was no more time to think about the past. I had a family to focus on. My daughters would be getting home soon, and after the day I'd had at the paralegal, I was definitely ready for a hug or two.

CHAPTER EIGHT

Over the next year or so, after my visit to the para-legal, I did everything I could to keep my daughters' lives as normal as possible. I also kept to my word, and I didn't accept any support payments from my ex once our divorce was finalized. When the girls needed anything, I knew that I could always count on him to pay his fair share. A simple phone call was all that was needed. When it was all said and done, our total combined legal bill was seven hundred and fifty dollars. The fact that my ex and I remained good friends throughout this whole process made the transition from being a wife to a single mom with three daughters a lot easier. I knew that my ex was struggling, as I was, to create his own identity as a single person in a world of couples.

Just as I had done after Bill's death, I spent a lot of time meditating and reading uplifting spiritual literature. I also took the time to reconnect with a lot of my old girl-friends. When I was married, my primary focus had been my husband and family, so this was an opportunity for me to just get out, catch up on girl talk, and have a few laughs. One friend that I made a conscious effort to see more of was a nurse by the name of Dianne. We'd become good friends since meeting and working together at a psychiatric hospital years earlier. Like Bill, it was her sense of humour that had initially drawn me to her, but her sense of caring and compassion made me truly cherish our friendship. Dianne and I began talking on the phone two or three times a week, which encouraged me on difficult days and cheered me on when things were going well. Dianne had a way of helping me see my glass as half full instead of half empty.

I didn't think anything of it when Dianne called me one evening near the end of June. Instead of us just chatting about work or how my girls were doing, she wanted to talk to me about a friend of hers named Adam. Dianne told me that he was a dentist and that they'd been friends for years. She also knew that he was going through a messy divorce and felt that he needed to vent his frustrations out to someone. Because of my recent experience with divorce, Dianne thought I might be able to give Adam some words of wisdom.

I was reluctant to get involved because I felt like a huge piece of my life had already been consumed by all of the toxic energy that accompanies divorce. Dianne was persistent, though, so grudgingly I took Adam's phone number from her and tried calling him from work. I wasn't sure what I was getting myself into, so I was relieved when I got his answering machine.

Adam returned my call, but over the next two weeks, we played telephone tag, trying to connect. Dianne finally decided that the only way this meeting was going to take place was to get us all together, so she planned an impromptu barbeque for the first Saturday in July. I arrived an hour earlier than Adam so I could have a good visit with Dianne. She must have thanked me ten times for doing this favour for her. "I know Adam will really appreciate talking to you, Molly," she said. "He's going through hell with his divorce. I just know you'll help him."

No matter what she said, I was still nervous, as I had very strong personal boundaries. Dianne reassured me and said, "Just counsel him like you would any other patient you were dealing with. The only difference here is that we're not at the hospital and we happen to be having a burger or two. In a few hours, it will all be over. Adam will feel better, you'll have done your good deed for the day, and then we'll all call it a night."

Just as Dianne went to the kitchen, Adam walked through the garden gate by the edge of Dianne's deck. He walked in like a man on a mission, past the many manicured gardens, directly over to where I was sitting. He introduced himself with a friendly smile, an outstretched hand, and a confident handshake. "You must be Molly," he said to me. "It's a pleasure to meet you. Dianne has told me nothing but good things about you."

Though I was aware that Adam was going through a rough divorce, he struck me as an easygoing, almost carefree individual. He wasn't wearing his insecurities or battle scars on his sleeve. I guessed him to be about six foot one, in his early forties, with an athletic build, deep blue eyes, and a slightly receding hairline. I was just about to offer him a drink when Dianne returned with three beers. She must have heard Adam talking to me while she was in the kitchen.

After giving Dianne a big hug Adam pulled up a chair and merged effortlessly into our conversation as if we'd all been friends for years. He was easy to talk to as long as the conversation revolved around superficial topics. Every time Dianne tried to focus the conversation on the real reason we'd gotten together, he would put up an emotional wall and go quiet.

"Adam, talk to Molly. She's helped other people going through divorce. Molly's divorced herself. She's trained in psychiatry. I asked her to come here tonight as a favour to me to try and help you. You've got to at least try." Even the pleadings of a good friend could not get him to open up. I sensed that Adam's outward confidence and warm smile were masking a Pandora's Box of inner pain.

After saying our good-byes to Dianne at the end of the evening, I walked with Adam out to our respective cars. It had been a long night, and I had to be at work early the next day. Standing by his car, Adam opened up just a little. "I'm sorry, Molly, if I wasted your time tonight," he said. "I know I need help with this. I want to open up, but it's so hard. It's so painful." Just saying that got him teary eyed and choked up. I could tell that he was feeling embarrassed at becoming emotional in front of a relative stranger, so I tried to put him at ease. I told him that when he was ready to talk, he should call Dianne. She would get a hold of me, and then I'd arrange for us to get together.

Driving home that night, I had second thoughts about what I'd said to Adam before I had left. What was I thinking, getting involved in a total stranger's divorce? I must be crazy! I was still trying to heal my own wounds; why would I take on someone else's baggage? Then it hit me—my problem, or gift, depending on how I looked at it, was that I was a nurse. I'd been trained all my life to be a giver, healer, and rescuer. Whatever you want to call it, it's all I'd ever known.

Much to my surprise, I received a phone call from Dianne the following Monday. She told me that Adam had contacted her and was inviting us both to his house the following Saturday for a barbeque. I reluctantly accepted the invitation, assuming that Adam had suddenly changed his mind and was now willing to open up to me about his divorce. I just hoped that I wasn't getting in over my head with a situation I knew virtually nothing about.

At Adam's the following week-end, we were greeted with that wide boyish grin and outstretched hand. Entering his front hallway, I noticed a number of pictures on the fireplace mantle of Adam with a little boy, whom I assumed was his son.

Adam, seeing that I had noticed the pictures, went over to the mantle, chose one of the picture frames, and showed it to me. "That's me and my son, Allan, at the beach," he said.

"How old is he?" I asked.

"He was five there, but he is six and a half now." While he was showing Dianne the same photograph, I browsed around the house. It was old and boxy looking but tastefully decorated.

Taking us on a tour of the house, Adam was a talkative tour guide. He told us all about the history of the home, the renovations he had done, and what he wanted to do in the future. Dianne and I were amazed that, at her house a week earlier, we had had trouble getting Adam to open up; now we couldn't get him to stop talking. Maybe this evening wouldn't be so bad after all. Maybe Dianne had exaggerated about the stress that Adam was under because of his divorce. Watching him parade around the house, I thought Adam looked the picture of happiness and contentment.

After finishing the main floor tour, Adam directed us towards a narrow curving staircase that led to the second floor. Adam, who'd been chatting steadily as he walked ahead of us up the stairs, suddenly hesitated and became silent as he reached the top of the landing. I watched him slowly take a deep breath before turning his head to the right and peering down a long, narrow hallway. As he walked towards the open door at the end of the hall, his confident swagger was gone. His shoulders sagged, and his gaze was focused on the floor at his feet, as if dreading every step toward the end of the hall. I had no idea what was behind that door, but something was very wrong. Adam had changed. Everything had changed.

CHAPTER NINE

As Dianne and I reached the open door and peered inside, we could see that it was a child's bedroom. The large dinosaur stuffed animal collection on the bed and the cars and trucks neatly arranged on top of the dresser made it easy to tell that it had been decorated for a little boy. I was struck by how perfect it looked, like a museum display rather than a typical little boy's room with books and toys on the floor and crayons on the desk. Everything was brand-new and untouched–even some of the stuffed animals still had their price tags attached.

The bedroom, for all its superficial beauty, was still missing the most important thing–a child to fill it with love and life. So where was his son? Why wasn't Allan here, spending time with his father? I had to find out, because it was obvious that Adam loved his little boy. Why would a father spend this kind of money just to have a "shrine" to a child rather than the child himself? I had so many questions. I prayed that I wasn't going to relive Bill's divorce all over again. One Barbara in a lifetime was enough for me.

I was about to ask Adam about his son when I saw him sit down on the edge of the bed, grab a stuffed animal off the pillow, and begin to wipe away tears from his face. On our first encounter at Dianne's, he'd been able to keep his emotions in check by filling the night air with idle chatter about things like the weather or politics, but now, in the security of his home and with friends around him, emotions overwhelmed his defences.

I went down the hall to get Adam some tissues and a cold face cloth. I could hear Dianne in the background, quietly talking to him, as I ran the cold water. I felt bad for Adam and his situation. It mirrored what I had already witnessed with both my friend Bill and my cousin Rick. Adam's pain wasn't any more intense than theirs; sadly, it seemed like the norm.

If history is the best teacher, then I'd definitely gained some insight into divorce. I was pretty sure I knew where Adam's scenario was headed. I didn't want to be the bearer of bad news, but I knew that someone was going to have to tell him the unfortunate truth; he'd be better off to just cut his losses, stop fighting, and move on with his life before being laid to waste by the family law industry like so many good father's before him. This industry has an insatiable appetite for the deep wallets of men who are naive enough to think they can defeat this Goliath. Anticipating that Adam would tell me that he was fighting either for custody of his son or for more access, I began to make my way back towards the bedroom.

Walking down the hall, I imagined a world where judges and lawyers were held accountable for their actions and decisions. Or better yet, I imagined how different the divorce process might be if these same decision makers had experienced divorce themselves prior to passing judgement upon others as to what is just and fair. Perhaps if lawmakers had personal insight into the devastation that divorce levels upon all families involved, decisions within family law would be made with more care and foresight.

Reaching the bedroom door, I switched my focus back to Adam before entering the room. Adam began apologizing to me for his emotional outpouring. "I'm so sorry, Molly," he said. "I don't know what came over me. I don't normally react that way when I come into my son's bedroom. I shouldn't be dumping my emotional baggage on you two. That wasn't my intention at all, honestly. I just wanted to share some good food and a few laughs with two really nice people. It gets kind of lonely sometimes, and walking into this empty bedroom, like I've done a million times before, made me realize just how alone I really am."

"Adam, listen to me," I said as I pulled up a chair and sat down. Dianne excused herself and went downstairs, closing the door as she left. "Don't ever apologize to me or anyone else for being human. I want you to know that my coming here tonight was never about a barbeque. Don't take this personally, but I couldn't care less about that. I came here because I care about you and what happens to you. I've seen so much pain because of divorce, and I'm not willing to sit on the sideline anymore and watch another man be taken down.

"Adam, my best friend, Bill, died in a car crash. His car swerved into a ditch, and he was killed instantly. He was going through a divorce, like you. I'll never know if he took his own life to end his pain and suffering or if it was truly just an accident. I tried so hard to help him get through that divorce. Now he's gone, but every day, I live with this nagging guilt that keeps saying, 'If I'd just talked to him a little longer, or maybe tried a little harder, then maybe, just maybe, my best friend would still be here today.'"

Now my eyes began welling up like Adam's had just minutes earlier. We were both mourning a loss. For me, it was Bill, and for Adam, it was his son. Adam leaned forward and pressed his forehead into mine for a moment–long enough for me to know that he understood my pain, just as I wanted to understand his. I gave him a genuine thank you as he handed me a tissue.

I regained my train of thought and continued. "Adam, I guess you can tell how passionate I am when it comes to the topic of divorce. Before we get into your story, I want to tell you about my Cousin Rick's divorce. Listen to my words carefully, because I guarantee you will learn a lot from what he went through. I can tell from your tears that you are in the midst of your own battle with your ex-wife. Hell, some people might call it a war. As you listen, ask yourself this one question: Is this the hill I want to die on? In other words, pick your battles carefully.

"My cousin couldn't, or, more precisely, wouldn't, turn the other cheek. He battled his ex for eighteen years. It's the most extreme case of legalized harassment against a man by his ex-wife and grown children that I have ever witnessed. It was bad enough that family law did nothing to stop his own family from destroying him; what's worse, no one did anything to protect his rights, because, where family law is involved, if you're a man, you don't have any.

"Before I begin Rick's story, let me ask you this: have you ever watched the Dickens movie called *A Christmas Carol*? It's the one where Ebenezer Scrooge is visited by the ghosts of Christmas past, present, and future."

"I love that movie," Adam said enthusiastically. "I watch it every Christmas Eve, without fail."

"Excellent! Well, here's my point. In that movie, Ebenezer is initially on a path to live a life of misery unless he can begin to make better life choices. As we all know, the ghosts helped him to see the error of his ways in one night, and he changed the direction of his life to one of joy and happiness. Both you and my cousin are like Ebenezer. Unfortunately for my cousin, he chose to stay on the path of most resistance, fighting all the way into his senior years. What was his ultimate reward for a life of wasted time and energy? I'll tell you: alcohol abuse, suicide attempts, ongoing bouts of depression, and an empty bank account.

"Think of me as one of those Christmas ghosts. By telling you Rick's story, I hope you'll choose to take a different path in your divorce by not engaging in the battle, not responding to the ongoing legal drama, and, most importantly, putting yourself first and just moving on with your life. Oh, and by the way, if you think I just ruined Rick's story by telling you the ending, don't worry–the middle is worse than the end."

CHAPTER TEN

I stopped to think of where I should start Rick's story. I could still hear the voice of my friend Bill saying, "Let the relationship stand the test of time." That was one of the most important insights he had shared with me concerning dating and marriage, so I figured that was a good place to start.

"Let me give you some background information, Adam, so you'll better understand why my cousin's divorce unfurled as it did. My cousin and Bill both made the same fatal mistake: They fell into lust, not love, and then rushed their relationships into marriage. In my cousin's case, he met and quickly married a pretty high school prom queen. I admit she was pretty to look at, but if he had taken the time to get to know her, he would have seen her controlling and obsessive side.

"I think the last smile I ever saw on Rick's face was on his wedding day, and I know the last decision he was ever allowed to make on his own was to say 'I do' at the altar. He didn't realize it at the time, but in terms of my psychiatric training, he had just married a lady with a personality disorder–PD for short. Some PD's are men, but according to most psychiatric literature, the majority of them are women. Many of the psychiatrists I trained under during my post-nursing education referred to these people as the closest thing to Satan on earth. They would often describe them as devoid of conscience, without the capacity to feel for anyone but themselves. Both male and female PD's tend to be very outwardly attractive, making them prime pick-up targets for the opposite sex.

"When you first meet PDs, they will come across as extremely charming and loving. They will adore others and worship them in the beginning, making them feel like kings or queens. Who wouldn't want to marry that? When they do marry the PDs, that's when the fairy-tale romance begins to unravel. Part of me feels sorry for these people because they've sentenced themselves to lives of hell, but another part of me says that they're getting what they asked for when they marry for looks alone. The best piece of advice I'd give any man or woman is to date your partner for years before making any sort of a commitment. If you're around this type of person long enough, their true colours will show. It takes a long time, and you've got to be patient, because these people can give Oscar-winning performances in the caring and compassionate department. They will put you on a pedestal as long as they believe that there is something for them to gain from the relationship, whether it is status or money.

"Once the wedding ring is on their finger, however, and their partner is committed to the relationship, everything changes. I've counselled hundreds of men and a few women who have lived with someone with a personality disorder, so it's easier for me to talk about male experiences, although the same things can apply to women.

"Men tend to tell me the same story. Each describes the feeling of suddenly waking up in the marriage to a wife he no longer knows. That sweet young thing he initially married has now transformed into a domineering, self-centred dictator. Where early in the marriage he could do no wrong, now he can do no right. Simply doing his best within the confines of the marriage is no longer good enough. He feels his self-esteem and confidence slowly being stripped away by a continual negative assault on his character. What he fails to realize is that his wife has always been a PD; she was simply waiting for the right time to blossom. Once the transformation is complete, she will demand her husband's undivided attention and adoration twenty-four hours a day. Everything is now about her—it always was; the man simply failed to see it. The female PD is materialistic and controlling in nature but doesn't expose that side of her personality until the man is so deep in the relationship that he can't escape without losing everything.

"If she decides that he is not living up to her expectations or that he is challenging her authority, he becomes expendable. Once the relationship reaches a point where she believes that the marriage has nothing more for her to gain by prolonging it, she will then focus her energy on controlling every asset accumulated during the marriage, including the children. The PD wife will rationalize her actions by telling herself that this is her rightful entitlement for having to put up with a less-than-perfect husband during the marriage. She honestly believes that the husband 'owes' her, and she will voice that opinion to anyone who will listen.

"Once a PD turns on someone, that person becomes the PD's primary focus. If they fight back, it only serves to strengthen the PD's resolve to fight harder until the person is affected at every level, from financial to emotional. Remember, these people are without conscience or remorse. The time it takes to win the game means nothing to PD's, be it a year or a lifetime. It's not about the money or the assets; it's about power and control. To them, winning is everything.

"The other thing about people with personality disorders is that they take their desires and emotions to the extreme. They'll seldom admit to being wrong, and they rarely accept blame or repercussions for their actions. If their lives are going badly, it's always because someone else has wronged them. They feel no remorse or guilt. For example, if there were six cookies on a plate and you took one, they'd take the other five. If you ask them why they didn't leave any, they'd look at you in utter disbelief and say, 'Because I was hungry.' They matter and you don't; that's the bottom line."

I stopped talking for a moment to see if Adam had any questions about what I had said. I could tell that he'd been listening, because even after I'd stopped talking, his head was still nodding up and down in agreement.

"Do you have any questions, Adam?" I asked. He just kept staring at me.

"Adam, are you there!" I said a little louder.

He jumped slightly as if startled, shook his head, and blurted out, "You just described my ex-wife! It's like you were living in my house!"

We sat for a moment staring at each other. What a breakthrough! He looked so happy. It was as if suddenly, everything he had gone through in his marriage finally made sense.

"Molly, she used to get up on her soapbox everyday and lecture me on why everything wrong in our marriage was my fault. She would always start with the same words: 'if you would just.' I'd always promise to try harder in order to save the marriage, though I felt my self-esteem slipping into obscurity. I'd sarcastically remark that only God is perfect and maybe she needed to take some responsibility for our marital problems. But you're right, Molly; in her mind, the only problem was me.

"I used to think I was losing my mind, living in that house with her. How could an intelligent man be wrong one hundred percent of the time? As a dentist, I felt valued by my patients and staff, yet as soon as I walked through the front door of our home, I'd be continually reminded of how far below the mark I was falling as both a husband and father. She would remark, 'Every time that I lower the bar on what I can expect from you, you surprise me by dropping the bar even lower.'

"Every time we went out, all I'd hear from our friends was, 'You must feel so lucky to be married to her because she's such a wonderful person.' I wanted to say, 'Then you try living with her,' but I kept those thoughts to myself. She needed constant praise and adoration to sustain her, to give her life, like a vampire needs blood. Like a vampire, she was a constant drain on my energy. If I gave her one hundred percent of my attention, she'd expect one hundred and ten. I'm so glad it's over, Molly. That relationship was killing me. Now that you've explained the concept of personality disorder to me, I'm starting to understand how I was being emotionally abused during my marriage. It didn't occur to me what was happening. She broke me down slowly. I felt like a prisoner of war with no escape. My self-esteem was shattered, and I just gave up trying to fight back, accepting both her portrayal of me as gospel, and a loveless marriage as my reality. I guess awareness of the problem is the first step in finding the solution, right?"

I tried to convey to Adam just how proud I was of him. It was great to see this broken man's confidence coming back. I was just starting to continue with Rick's story when Adam piped in. "Molly, I'm sorry for butting in, but you've been so good to me that I just want to be honest with you." His voice got a little quieter as he went on. "I feel a little bit embarrassed telling you this after everything you've talked about, but I'm afraid that you can put me in the same category as both Bill and your cousin Rick."

"Oh no, not you, too," I laughed, trying to make light of an awkward moment for him.

"Oh, yes, Molly, I also went for the pretty package. You know, if I'd only taken the time to open it, I probably would have smelled the rotten eggs inside." We both broke into laughter.

"Adam, let me reassure you about something. I'm not here to judge you in any way for decisions you made in your past. I simply want to make sure that you make better decisions in the future, especially concerning how you handle your divorce proceedings. I'll bet that because of what you went through in your own marriage, you think you know how my cousin's marriage unfolded, don't you? Well, don't get ahead of yourself. You may know the wrath of an angry ex-wife from your own experience, but each marriage is different and each woman is unique.

"My cousin will attest to that fact. He has an amazing sense of humour. If he were here right now sitting with us, he'd tell you that you haven't lived until you've witnessed his ex-wife in action and with all the blessings of our family court system. Remember, it's not in the listening that this story is life changing, but rather in the learning."

"I'm all ears," Adam said eagerly.

With that, I began. "My cousin and I are more alike than we would ever care to admit. We both have feisty Irish tempers and can be bull-headed, but one thing we are not is mean-spirited. Sure, we may be quick to anger, but we're even quicker to forgive. What I'm trying to say is that we would never go out of our way to intentionally hurt someone. In fact, the opposite is true. We go out of our way to help others–it doesn't matter if you are a friend, family member, or total stranger. If you are in need and I have it to give, it's yours. Rick is the same way.

"That's why it was so hard for me to watch what Rick went through after marrying Donna. Throughout the marriage, he always put the needs of the family ahead of his own. He worked as a machinist and was the sole provider for the family. He often worked double shifts so the family could have the best of everything. Their two children were never denied access to any extracurricular activity they chose to participate in. My cousin, on the other hand, was so busy making money for others to spend that he rarely had time for himself, his buddies, or any hobbies. He would have been okay with that if he'd had a safe and peaceful home to live in, but according to him, peaceful it was not.

"Even while he was working up to sixteen hours a day, often six or seven days a week, Rick said that his wife still managed to raise issues to fight over. He told me that her 'nothing is ever good enough' attitude, as he describes it, started taking its toll on him. The first casualty according to Rick was his sense of humour, followed quickly by him becoming extremely quiet and submissive at home. He said he began to speak to his wife only when she spoke to him directly. By the time he got home from work, he was too tired to do battle with her, so he said that it was just easier to give up trying in order to keep the peace.

"When he was young, girls were attracted to Rick not only because of his good looks but because he was also charismatic. The stress associated with the marriage, however, started to age him. Now, after eighteen years of fighting his divorce, I hardly recognize him. I can only imagine what he'd look like today and where his health might be if he'd stopped responding, stopped fighting years ago, and simply moved on with his life."

Adam nodded in agreement but didn't speak, as he didn't want to interrupt my train of thought.

"According to Rick, Donna liked to call and check up on him everywhere he went. He said that she knew his work schedule better than he did, making him accept every extra shift he was offered, no matter how tired he was. There was never enough money to satisfy her. He said jokingly that things had gotten so bad that he wouldn't have been surprised to learn that she had calculated how long it should take him to drive home from work. Heaven help him if he stopped somewhere for a beer or two. If he did, he knew exactly what the drill at home would be. He said that he would receive a guilt trip for putting his needs ahead of his family, whom, she would say, had been waiting patiently for him at home. In order to keep the peace and survive in the marriage, he said that he learned to accept the fact that the only freedom he was going to get was the time he spent alone in the car driving to and from work.

"The remarkable thing about my cousin is that, throughout all this emotional blackmail, he never said a bad word to the children about their mother. He loved his kid's and didn't want to tarnish their opinion of her. Eventually, though, he reached his limit of being controlled, and he rebelled. He was physically burned out from all the extra shifts at work and decided to turn one down and just enjoy himself one evening by watching some sports on television at a friend's house. Donna warned him, telling him that if he chose time with his friend over work, she would terminate the marriage. He remained defiant, and the evening ended with Rick taking his personal belongings, which had been stuffed into two garbage bags, out of the garage, vowing never to set foot in that house again. This is where the story really gets ugly."

CHAPTER ELEVEN

"After Rick left and the divorce was initiated, he told me that both of his children suddenly turned against him and that he believed his wife had something to do with it, although he couldn't prove it for sure. In psychiatry, there is a term for this–parent alienation." I hoped Adam would pay particular attention to this next part, because I suspected this was what he was going through with his son and ex-wife.

This alienation usually occurs within the context of a custody battle and is defined as the "programming" of a child by a parent into a campaign of denigration against the other parent, without justification. This programming can be deliberate, arising out of a malicious attempt to hurt the other parent and gain control, or it can just evolve naturally out of the dynamics of the divorce.

Rick's friends told him that the story circulating around was that he had simply up and left, abandoning his family in the middle of the night, and that his wife was acting like his leaving was a total shock to her. Rick understood, under those circumstances, how his children

could come to view him as the bad guy who had aban-
doned them and hurt the mother they loved. Unfortunately for Rick, both children broke off all contact with
him before ever giving him the chance to tell his side of
the story.

Psychiatrists will tell you that if you hear something
often enough, it will eventually become your reality. This
is great if you are repeatedly telling a child something
positive such as, "You will accomplish anything you put
your mind to." Who knows what was reinforced in the
childrens' minds about their father behind closed doors
and in his absence? If it was something along the lines of
"Your father must not love you, because he left us," then
it would only make sense that their reality would become
one of anger.

The reality for Rick was that at about the same time
that the divorce proceedings started, an unprovoked
campaign of harassment was launched against him. He
suspected that his ex-wife and children might be behind
it, but once again, he couldn't prove it. He wanted to be
wrong on this one. They wouldn't do such things, he
kept telling me, not against the man who had faithfully
taken his family on expensive vacations each year, constantly worked double shifts, given all his money to the
family so that no one had ever gone without and who
was so determined not to hurt anyone that he shielded
his own children from his emotional abuse so they would
always view their mother in a positive light. According to
Rick, he found glue in his car locks, loosened lug nuts on
his car tires, not to mention the forty pounds of animal
excrement he found dumped on his car.

Rick said that what his family did do, however, was yell obscenities at him in public whenever they saw him and harass his other family and friends, phoning them at all hours of the night and day to tell them what a horrible person he was. And he said it didn't stop there. Donna accused him of stealing their children's college-fund money, so his whole family resorted to picketing outside his work carrying signs that read something to that effect. It even made the front page of the local newspaper.

Rick moved to a new city to escape the harassment. He attempted to settle down into the quiet life he had always dreamed of, but it was not to be. He wasn't going to escape that easily. It was bad enough that his ex kept taking him back to court, asking for more money, but she also persuaded the children to start filing suits against their father, independent of her claims. He kept hiring lawyers to fight these attacks, which ended up being financial suicide for him.

Somewhere in all this confusion, he managed to meet and marry his true soul mate, Beth. Their happiness was short lived, as this union gave his ex-wife another avenue for financial attack. My cousin was paying his monthly spousal and child support payments faithfully, but every year, Donna made him verify his yearly income with her lawyer. Soon after he said "I do" to Beth, his ex-wife took him back to court.

Donna's lawyer argued that Rick now had a higher standard of living than his ex-wife because his new wife was working full-time. Donna's lawyer soon made sure that she got a big slice of Rick and Beth's hard-earned financial pie every month. The court started calculating Rick's spousal support based on their joint income, which in essence financially penalized Rick's new wife for falling in love and marrying a divorced man. She was forced to give up a portion of her monthly income to financially support a woman she barely knew. It made no difference to the courts that she was already supporting her own four children from a previous marriage.

Every year, Rick and Beth were dragged back into court to have support payments calculated and re-calculated. His new wife eventually quit the job that she had loved for many years. For Beth, the stress associated with having her privacy violated every year by having to let a lawyer peruse her financial statements was one thing, but the rage she felt towards Rick's ex-wife was beyond words. To add salt to her wounds, the court wouldn't even allow Rick to transfer his life insurance policy from his ex-wife to her. To his ex, Rick was worth more dead than alive, and Beth worried every day that if this ongoing harassment weren't stopped, Donna would eventually get her wish. Unfortunately for my cousin, that wish nearly came true.

Nothing prepared me for the phone call I got approximately five years after Rick's divorce from Donna. After taking the call, I quietly sat at my kitchen table and relived many of the same emotions I had felt after getting the call about Bill's death years earlier. I was told that a car had struck down Rick and that he was in intensive care with multiple fractures. I was hours away from the hospital, so there was nothing I could do at that moment except pray for his recovery. The good news was that the police had arrested a suspect at the scene. The bad news was that the suspect was his son, Tim.

When I got to the hospital, Beth was sitting at Rick's bedside, gently caressing his hand as he slept. When she saw me, she broke down in tears. "Oh Molly," she said, "his own son tried to kill him! Why? Rick hasn't had any contact with him for five years. What would motivate him to do that?"

I didn't know what to say, so I just said nothing, choosing instead to simply hug her and let her know that I was there for them both.

"Molly, I didn't want to leave him alone, but now that you're here, would you mind if I grab a quick bite to eat in the cafeteria? I haven't had anything all day."

"Sure," I said, "you go ahead. I just want a few moments alone with Rick, then I'll come and find you." Beth gave me another quick hug, and then she was gone.

I stood in Rick's room, looking at all the tubes snaking their way in and out of his body, and listening to the beeps and sounds of machines that surrounded his bed. I began to get angry. The question I wanted answered wasn't about the motivation behind this tragedy, but rather, why nothing had been done to prevent things from escalating to this point.

Sitting in the chair at the head of his bed, I began gently running my fingers through my cousin's hair to comfort him. I studied his face, and for the first time, I saw just how much the ongoing harassment had aged him. That aside, he still looked like an angel to me as he slept. Watching his heartbeat dance across the heart monitor, I still wondered how a person could purposefully hurt someone else and still be able to live free of guilt or remorse. This man had only asked for peace in life, yet all he had received was torment because of divorce and a family that had turned against him without justification.

When he had first been subjected to this harassment, Rick had done everything he could to stop it. He'd filed complaints with the police department, but he hadn't been taken seriously. They had said there was nothing they could do unless they caught the person involved in the act. They had gone so far as to say that if it really was his ex-wife or one of their kids responsible for the harassment, they were probably just having a bad day and that everything would look better in the morning. In other words, his fears and concerns were brushed off.

Society doesn't care if a man is being harassed or even abused. If it did, we'd have shelters for men. Until we exhibit equal concern for men and women concerning this issue, no one will ever change my opinion. No one cared that each time Rick's property was damaged, it was costing him money or thought of the toll on his health and reputation each time he was either publicly or privately harassed. It wouldn't be fair to lay all the blame at the feet of the police department; there's more than enough blame to go around. Not once did any court-appointed official do anything to help this man. No judge or lawyer ever heard his pleas for help; they were all too busy turning their backs on him and walking away.

Rick didn't fare any better when it came to the financial harassment. No matter how trivial the allegations against him were, he still ended up in court, having to prove his innocence and he wasn't allowed to represent himself. With a four-hundred-dollar-per-hour lawyer at his side, he was definitely in a no-win situation. Donna was never obliged to prove that her allegations were true, but Rick constantly had to prove that these same allegations were false. If he failed to do so, it usually resulted in another hit to his dwindling bank account. The ironic thing was that once he had proven that her allegations were false and that she had, in fact, committed perjury, Donna was not punished by the court and Rick had no legal recourse by which he could be compensated for his time, financial expenses or all the stress placed on his health.

I felt myself getting even angrier about how unfair our legal system is when it comes to men's rights. Where else but in family law could a woman commit perjury and get away with it? If you view divorce as an industry, like I do, then you realize that the end result of guilt or innocence holds far less importance than the process itself. It is the process of law that makes lawyers and judges rich. Confrontation is the financial bread and butter of the legal world. It's in the best interest of everyone employed within the court system to hear each and every allegation put forth by an angry ex-wife, no matter how frivolous.

If these emotionally charged divorced women are allowed to recklessly accuse within the confines of our courts without fear of repercussions, they'll keep coming back. It's no different than the business plan of a good restaurant. If you can encourage your customers to keep eating at your establishment, you make more money. The last thing a restaurant owner wants is for his or her customers to have bad experiences. It's not rocket science. No customers means no money. No money means no jobs. The court system is no different; judges and lawyers have families to support and bills to pay, just like everyone else.

Once you grasp that concept, you can understand why legalized harassment has to be an integral part of the divorce process. This industry has to make profits to survive, and allowing women to harass men is the best means to that end. It keeps a steady flow of conflict and money pouring into the court system, keeping multitudes of people employed, from the security guard at the court entrance to the court stenographer; right up to the judge's themselves.

The more I thought about this concept of legalized harassment, the more impressed I was with the ingenuity of our legal system. Allowing indiscriminate harassment of men by ex-wives to fill the court's financial coffers was one thing, but it's the feeling of power that women have in court that keeps many of them coming back for more.

For some women, this ongoing harassment offers them, possibly for the first time in their lives, the chance to experience what it feels like to have ultimate power and control over their ex-husbands. For some women, you can't put a price on that experience. Sure, they may have to cough up some support dollars to enjoy the show, but who cares; the next cheque is probably on its way.

My thoughts suddenly drifted away from anger and back to my cousin as he began to tussle around in the bed. He was too sedated with pain and sleeping medication to know what he was doing. The poor guy was just a jumble of wires, tubes, and casts. I pulled the blanket up over his shoulders, tucking it under the mattress on both sides, like a mother would do to comfort a sick child.

I thought of how needless this tragedy was. Rick's son had been such a beautiful little boy. During the marriage, Rick and Donna's house had overflowed with pictures of this smiling little boy and his father together. Anyone who saw these photos always commented on the obvious love between them. Even though I was well aware of parent alienation and how it can occur, I had always thought that it was something that happened to other people's children. But when my cousin had told me how his own son had treated him with absolute contempt in public, then I had truly understood the power that one parent can have over the mind of an impressionable young child. It was still no excuse for what Tim had done to his father. He couldn't use alienation as a defence for attempted murder. He was old enough to choose communication over violence, and now he was looking at a life behind bars. I prayed to God, asking him to help me work through my anger and come to a place within myself where I could forgive Tim, because right now, I hated him.

It hadn't been only Tim in the car that day; family law had been a co-conspirator. If I am being abused and report it to the authorities and they do nothing, should they not be held accountable when their next encounter with me is to pick up what's left of my bruised and battered body? How is this any different? My cousin told the courts that he was being forced out of his children's lives, leaving them captive with a woman whom he felt had made it her mission to erase any love these children had in their hearts for their father. Why hadn't the courts taken his allegations seriously? Was it because he was just another one of those angry men, as the feminists would have you believe, or is there a deeper problem that involves "reverse" discrimination of men in court?

I wished that I could put family law on trial. It had robbed my cousin of his children and destroyed his health. It had taken away years of his life that he could never get back. But worst of all, it had stolen his laughter and ability to feel joy. I know that even family law can't destroy a man's soul, but it had definitely put Rick's on life support. With those thoughts, I gently leaned over, kissed Rick on the forehead, and whispered in his ear, "You are so loved," before leaving him to go find Beth.

CHAPTER TWELVE

I found Beth sitting alone in the farthest corner of the cafeteria with a vending-machine sandwich, a half eaten donut, and an untouched cup of coffee in front of her. She was so exhausted that she didn't notice me until I sat in the chair next to her. When she turned and saw me, she leaned into my arms and began crying. I held and rocked her like a baby while telling her to let it out, as I was there for her.

Each time I began to loosen my embrace so I could talk to her, she would cling to me even tighter. Now with a family member she trusted, the tough facade that she had put on for her husband dissolved. She tried to speak, but all she could muster were choppy, incoherent phrases and mournful cries. I finally peeled her arms from around my neck and gently nudged her back into the chair so we could talk. She looked at me through blood-shot eyes, smiling faintly to let me know that she was relieved I was there. She felt safe with me because she knew that I loved her with the same intensity that I loved my cousin. I sat and waited as she composed both herself and her thoughts. Then she began to talk.

"We made a pact that morning over breakfast that nothing was going to spoil our day together, not even the fact that Rick had to see his lawyer again. Donna had just launched another round of allegations against him, but even that didn't seem to faze him. He was determined to stay positive, even clicking his coffee mug against mine in order to seal the deal. So off we went to the park to spend our day walking hand in hand, talking, enjoying the scenery and listening to the birds. It was beautiful, Molly. For those few hours, Rick was his old self again, beaming with happiness as he told me one corny joke after another. I remember thanking God for giving me back my husband, the one with the beautiful sense of humour. Why did his son take that away from me, Molly? Why! I feel so guilty. If only I hadn't driven him to the lawyer's office on that day...maybe...just maybe..."

Beth's final words trailed off into tears as she once again wrapped her arms around me and began to cry. I knew that one of us had to remain strong, but why did it have to be me? I felt selfish. I wanted someone to just hold me so I could let out what I was feeling inside. I kept fighting the urge to break down, but it was so hard. That was my cousin lying there helpless in that hospital bed. My own flesh and blood! The rage I felt inside was churning my stomach to the point of nausea. Somehow, I had to let my anger go. There would be time for me to deal with my feelings later, but right now, I had to help Beth.

"It's not your fault, Beth. There's nothing you could have done differently. Don't blame yourself, please."

"Molly, I sensed a change in Rick's mood as soon as we got in the car, left the park, and started driving towards the lawyer's office. God bless him. He was still trying to keep to his word and remain positive, but I could sense the stress in his words as he talked. Who can blame him? Donna never gives this man a moment of peace. He's like a soldier in battle who's always looking over his shoulder, or sleeping with one eye open because he doesn't know how, when, or where the next assault will occur.

"By the time we got to the strip mall where the lawyer's office was located, he was in a full-blown state of agitation. He just wanted to get this meeting over with. Unfortunately, there was construction going on near the entrance to the office. Instead of letting me find a way to let him off near the door, he decided to jump out of the car and walk across the construction area instead.

"Don't try and drive up to the entrance," he said. "I'll meet you at this same spot in twenty minutes. You can't miss me. I'll be the tall, good-looking guy with his thumb out waiting for a ride."

"He gave me a playful wink and a peck on the cheek before jumping out of the car and heading out across the construction area. I decided to drive to the far side of the mall and do a little shopping in the drugstore. After twenty minutes, I drove back to our meeting spot, but Rick wasn't there. I wasn't worried because I assumed that his meeting was running late. Then I saw him.

"He was propped up against a light post near the entrance to the lawyer's office. A large group of people had gathered around Rick and were pointing towards a car that was parked nearby. There was a lot of commotion, and I could hear people screaming for someone to call the police and an ambulance.

I don't remember much of what happened next. It was surreal, as if my life was moving in slow motion. I remember hearing the sound of gravel under my feet as I ran towards Rick. My lungs ached for oxygen, but I couldn't get to him fast enough. I pushed my way through the crowd until I was face-to-face with Rick.

"He tried to kill me, Beth!" gasped Rick. "My son, Tim! He tried to kill me! I saw his face just before the car hit me! Why!? Why!? Someone please help me! My god, the pain is so bad!"

"I wanted to walk towards him, but I couldn't move," Beth continued. "It was as if my feet were suddenly made of stone and all the blood had drained from my body. I could hear Rick's words, but they weren't registering. My whole world was spinning out of control. I felt sick. I was in shock. You can't describe the agony you feel watching the man you love writhe in pain, knowing that you are powerless to stop it. I felt so sorry for him, Molly. His body and clothes were covered in blood, and his shorts were torn and pulled partway down his legs. With every breath he took, he would double over in pain.

"It took me a few seconds to pull myself together, and then I rushed to his side. I was afraid to touch him.

He was badly injured, and I didn't want to put him in more pain. His colour didn't look good, and he was slowly going into shock from the pain and blood loss. The best thing I could do was keep him awake by talking to him and reassuring him until paramedics came. Once the ambulance arrived, they quickly started working on Rick. Once I felt secure that he was in safe and capable hands, I was ready to deal with Tim. Everyone standing there knew by the expression on my face that I wanted to face my husband's attacker."

"He's over here," I heard a man say in a husky voice."

"I walked around to the far side of the car and found Tim, still pinned to the front of the car by two men who had pulled him from the driver's seat and were now holding him, waiting for the police to arrive. It was hard to even look at him. I wanted him to rot in jail for the rest of his miserable life. I walked up and put my face inches from his so that he could see the pain in my eyes. With teeth clenched, I said only one word: Why? The coward that he was, he wouldn't even own up to what he had done to his own father."

"The car just lurched forward," he whimpered. "I think something in the engine must have broken. I didn't do anything."

"Both of the men holding him began to shake their heads in unison. They were shocked by his brazen arrogance. One of them started to talk and told me a very different story."

"I saw the whole thing," he said. "At first I thought it was just some kid burning rubber with his car, or someone gunning to beat a yellow light. I tried to pick out what direction the noise was coming from. Your husband had just left the mall and was beginning to walk towards me. I watched in shock as he suddenly turned his attention to his right, just in time to see a car bearing down on him at full speed. At first he didn't look that concerned since the parking lot was almost empty. I watched him step back to let the car go by, but suddenly it turned and came toward him once again. He was a sitting duck with nowhere to run. The last thing I saw was your husband shaking his fist at the driver just seconds before it hit him.

He paused to catch his breath and continued. "I'll never forget the thud of metal as the car slammed into his body and dragged him under the wheels. Before I realized what was going on, I heard the sound of the transmission click into reverse and saw the car begin backing up. The tires rolled slowly over his body, crushing his bones like eggshells. I started screaming and running towards the car. As I reached it, I heard the transmission click into gear yet again. That bastard wasn't finished yet! I pounded on the trunk as hard as I could and tried to get a hold of the bumper to stop the car, but was it was hopeless. It slowly inched forward to try and crush him again.

"I don't know where this guy standing beside me came from, but between the two of us, we were somehow able to pull this guy out of the car and wrestle him to the ground. I moved the car off your husband, and when I first laid eyes on him, I thought for sure he was dead. He's one tough guy. He was still conscious but coughing up blood on the pavement. We decided to prop him up against a light pole. It may not have been the smartest thing to do, but it was better than letting him choke to death on his own blood."

"Just as I started to thank them both profusely for helping my husband, the police arrived," said Beth. "An officer stepped in and gently pulled me away from the car.

"Don't worry, he assured me, your husband is getting the best care possible. I just spoke with the paramedics. If you don't mind giving me your car keys, an officer will drive your car back to your house. You can sit in the back of the ambulance with your husband for the ride back to the hospital. We'll be sure to let your family know what's happened.

"As I walked toward the ambulance, I paused and watched with relief as an officer was in the process of handcuffing and placing Tim in the backseat of his cruiser. Once in the car, he looked out the window just long enough for our eyes to meet. Attempting to kill his father was frightening enough, but what made my blood run cold was the look of pride on his face as they drove him away.

"I don't know what I'd do if I ever lost Rick, Molly. Seeing him helpless in that hospital bed made me realize that nothing else matters more than relationships. The doctors tell me that he's going to live, but I guess that depends on what your definition of living is. Will we spend the rest of our life looking over our shoulders, waiting for his son, daughter, or maybe even his ex-wife to finish him off? If they can't get to him, will I be next? Will he be crippled for life? I think that I'm a good Christian. I have always done my best to turn the other cheek when someone wrongs me, but this is so hard. It was his son! I don't understand this."

Beth's cell phone rang; it was her daughter Jenna. I sensed relief in her voice as she explained to her daughter that Rick was going to live. I could hear Jenna telling her mother that she was just parking the car downstairs and that she would be up in about five minutes. With that, I got up and gave Beth one last big hug. She needed time with her daughter, and I needed time alone.

As I had continued with Rick's story, Adam could see that I needed a moment to shake off the events of that day. He himself was in disbelief.

"Molly, I still can't believe what happened. I mean, a son running over his own father. That's just unheard of."

"Well, Adam, it was quite the story. It even made it's way into the local newspaper. I guess you could say that my cousin got his five minutes of fame, but definitely not for the right reasons."

Adam chuckled. He could tell that I was now in a better frame of mind, so he pressed me to continue with my story. "So what did you do after leaving the hospital? Where did you go to be alone?"

"Well, Adam, the magnitude of what had happened to my cousin was beginning to sink in. It was time for me to have a good talk with God, and I knew just the place to go. I like to retreat back to a place where I feel safe when I need time to think things through. The hospital was just a twenty-minute car ride to the cemetery where both of my parents were buried, so that's where I headed to talk with my parents and God at the same time. I wasn't going to find a safer spot than that.

I pulled in and parked to the left of where my parents had been laid to rest. In life, I had been able to talk to them about anything, and today would be no different. It had been so many years since they both had died, but I always sensed their presence with me every time I stood at their gravesite. I got down on my hands and knees and started clearing away the weeds and grass that had grown up around their markers.

It had been too long since my last visit. They'd both given me so much in life that I was determined to always give them respect in death. When I was a little girl, I could never have imagined that my parents, vibrant and full of life, would one day be gone, reminding me that life is but a blink, and then it's over.

I closed my eyes and ran my fingertips over every letter of their names, like a blind person reading brail. I tried to visualize the sights, smells, and sounds that I associated with each of them. Like a gentle caress of my face, by my mother, as she tucked me in at night, smiling at me with a look of unconditional love. Or the quiet, unspoken love of my father, where a hot meal on the table, a gentle rub of my head, or an invitation to go fishing on a Saturday morning was always his way of saying "I love you."

The emptiness of the cemetery resonated with the emptiness within my heart. It was hard to comprehend that my parents' lives had, in the end, been reduced to nothing more than a few old photographs, some mementos, and their names carved onto a piece of cold stone. I could hear God's voice saying, "If you don't utilize the gift of foresight, all you're left with is the curse of hindsight." How many people spend their whole lives saying "I wish I had" rather than "I'm glad I did"? I was no different. There I was, on my hands and knees, wishing for one more moment in my mother's arms or just one chance to smell my dad's cooking again as he stood guard over his pots. People look at the world so differently. For me, I felt cheated out of a father who was taken too soon. In Tim's world, he also felt cheated, but for a father who wasn't taken soon enough.

I could feel my body beginning to stiffen from being in the same position for too long. I stood up and brushed the grass and dirt from the knees of my pants. It was hard for me to believe that I was only a few years younger than my mother had been when she had died. I began meandering among the gravestones and thinking about some of the things my parents had taught me.

My father taught me about the commitment that accompanies marriage. On his wedding day, he said his vows in front of my mother and before God, swearing to always take care of her until she took her last dying breath. He never broke that promise. I never saw a man love a woman more than my dad loved my mother. He taught by example that the true joy of marriage is only achieved by giving of oneself and one's love, without expectations or the need for praise. When my mother got sick with a brain tumour, my father could have walked out on her. He could have viewed her as a burden and said things like "Why me?" or "What about my needs?" He understood that marriage isn't about convenience or giving up because you don't like the cards life has dealt you. It's about keeping your word. Because of that, when things got tough, he loved her even more. At the end of her life, she left this world with her hand in his, her dignity intact. No words were spoken. Words weren't needed. Their bond was love. They both knew it because they had lived it.

In childhood, my mother taught my six older siblings and me a very important lesson. She used to say that happiness is something you are, rather than something you buy. I remember coming home one day after playing down the street at the Reids' house with their two daughters. These two kids had every toy imaginable, but their father travelled all over the world for business and was rarely home. When I told her that it would be great to have all those toys, she turned to me and said, "Your father and I can give you five dollars for a toy and tell you to run along, or we can give you our time. Which is more valuable to you? And while we're at it, Molly, ask yourself what you think those two girls really need and want from life–another toy, or time with their father." I had scratched my head at first, but soon, I had figured out what she was teaching me. You can love a toy, but it will never love you back. Only a parent can do that. That's why spending quality time with both parents is essential.

The other great teacher in childhood was observation. My parents were married for many years, and there was the odd occasion when I witnessed them having an argument. However, the beautiful thing about them was that even in the heat of battle, they never lost sight of just how much they loved each other. Because of that, they never purposely hurt each other in any way, like people do today. I'll never forget the words they had hanging on the wall beside their bed throughout their whole marriage: "Never go to bed angry." They lived by that rule. My mother told me that the key to a long and happy marriage is to marry your best friend, like she had. My father said that you always have to work together as a team. If you focus on each other's strengths, you will bring out the best in each other. If you focus on the weaknesses, you will tear your relationship apart. Most important to my father was respect for your partner. Without that, he said, even the best marriage will end in failure.

My parents were, by far, my best teachers. If they were alive today, they would both be heartbroken by the cruelty that so often accompanies marriage breakdown. I chuckled to myself as I pictured my mother talking to a present-day divorce lawyer. This was a woman who didn't have a mean bone in her body, so I could see the puzzled look on her face as she questioned the lawyer's motives. "Please explain to me again,' she would say "why the law gives me the right to hurt my husband intentionally, to take his money and everything he worked for, leaving him struggling to survive? Even if I hated him, I wouldn't be capable of doing that. We both gave one hundred percent to the marriage and the children. We considered it an equal partnership. Why do I get preferential treatment over him? I must be missing something. I just don't get it."

I was still chuckling as I walked back over to my parents' grave. I read their names out loud, "Rubin and Marie Murphy." I missed them so much and was beginning to believe that they were the ones in the better place. They were together in love, for all eternity, not stuck here in this cesspool of greed and anger. When my time comes to take my last breath, I can guarantee that no one will see me fighting to stay here. My godfather always told me that by the end of your life, you'd be able to count the number of people on one hand you were able to trust during your lifetime. I used to scoff at this notion, but after my experience in the paralegal office and seeing what Bill and Rick's ex-wives had done to them, I wasn't laughing anymore.

CHAPTER THIRTEEN

I started walking along one of the many laneways that weaved through the cemetery landscape. I made my way towards a large pond and, once there, sat down by the water's edge. The sunlight sparkled off the water's surface, smooth as a sheet of glass. I looked around. It was just God and I. I felt safe there. I began to talk.

I asked God to envelope me in his love. I told him how I was hurting inside and desperately wanted to believe that there still was goodness in this world but I just couldn't see it anymore. I remember going to church as a little girl and being taught that to always give love is the definition of success in God's eyes–to treat others the way you want to be treated. Back then it was a spiritual moral that everyone aspired to live by. Sadly, those beautiful words now had no meaning. "Treat others the way you want so that you can come out on top" had now, in my opinion, become a more accurate depiction of our self-absorbed society.

I looked at divorce. I didn't want to stereotype women as always being the bad guys, but I could only speak from personal experience. When I had gone to see the paralegal, I could have buried my ex financially, ensuring that I would come out on top, but I had a conscience. I treated him with the same respect and dignity that I would have asked for had I been the one walking in his shoes. Every woman who has ever gone through divorce makes a personal choice. They have all had to ask themselves if they would succumb to the greed that lawyers and courts are willing to place at their feet or if they would listen to their conscience–or spiritual compass, as I like to call it–and accept only what they truly need. I had chosen the latter. Like my mother, even if I had hated my ex at the end, I couldn't have hurt him. But apparently, a lot of women can. I just had to look at what Bill's wife had done to get his money both before and after he died. My cousin was in a hospital bed because his ex treated him with contempt and had turned his own children against him, all for the sake of money.

When I stood by my parents' grave, I could still sense the depth of the love they had for one another. In their day, divorce was almost unheard of. I asked God what was happening to the institution of marriage. I said that it was dying right in front of our eyes. Back in my parents' day, saying "I do" had really meant something, but now we are living in a disposable society, where convenience is everything. Now, when something gets old or begins to break down, we don't even think of fixing it; we just throw it away and get a new one. This has become our philosophy for marriage, especially when fifty percent of all marriages are ending in divorce.

I believed then, and I still believe now, that our divorce laws have made it too easy and too lucrative to throw in the towel at the first sign of trouble in a marriage, especially if you're a woman. I know, because I went through divorce. With our court's no-fault divorce, I didn't even have to give any specific reason why our marriage was over, other than the standard "irreconcilable differences," which basically covered everything. With the money that family law was willing to help me take from my ex-husband's bank account every month, "lucrative" would have been an understatement.

I told God how unfair the system is, how it makes sure that men are left so powerless and broke that they can't afford to have voices in court. They can fight in court and starve or accept their fate in silence and hope their ex-wives' financial sweet tooth is satisfied. Women know that they have the upper hand over men. The courts have ensured it. If I decide to get divorced, I don't even have to be fair or nice in the process. I'll get what I want either way. For that reason alone, it would be a rare sight these days to find a woman who is committed enough to her husband and marriage, like they were in my mother's day, to put in the time and effort needed to save the relationship.

Our family courts have turned divorce into a passive game for the woman and a futile fight for survival for the man. The woman simply engages a lawyer to do her bidding, then waits and watches as her ex squirms under the scrutiny of the courts. I told God that I had no problem with divorce as a means of ending a marriage that wasn't salvageable, but what I couldn't accept was someone making a decision to purposely and permanently hurt his or her ex-spouse by either leaving them with no money or assets, or denying them access to their own children.

It was just my opinion, but I told God that I believed that everything in life comes down to two key ingredients: choice and conscience. Everything we say or do in life comes down to choice, and what choice we ultimately make depends on whether we have a conscience. This holds true in any instance, whether it is how we interact with others, raise our children, view marriage, or conduct ourselves during divorce.

I don't expect everyone to believe in God, because that's a personal choice. But as a society, I feel that if we didn't believe in anything greater than ourselves or hold people accountable for their actions, then society as we know it, would be devoid of conscience. If the concept of a heaven holds no value within society either, people will only live for the here and now, regardless of who gets hurt along the way. When you see "for sale" signs on church lawns and empty pews on Sundays, it gets you thinking. They don't allow the Lord's Prayer in schools anymore because they don't want to offend anyone, and Sunday is no longer a day of worship. The malls are crammed with eager Sunday shoppers looking to buy another material possession they really don't need. When I connected the dots that day, there was only one conclusion: We are living in a godless society. I just had to look at the world around me.

I asked God what had happened to loving your fellow man. I have been in court with my cousin for moral support and watched his own children hiss at and heckle him. I have listened to the pain in my cousin's voice as he talked of the wife he once loved and how she had accused him of hideous things in court. I have seen my cousin's son smile at the prospect of having possibly killed his father. I have held my best friend as he wept after his ex-wife denied him access to his own children and looked on as the courts did nothing to enforce his rights as a father. I ended up burying him because of divorce and then stood by and watched his hypocritical "grieving" widow attempt to steal his parents' company for all its cash value.

What about the children of divorce? I talked to God about that, too. What would be their fate? These children aren't allowed to speak. The courts speak for them, invoking the phrase "It's in the best interest of the children" like some sort of catch phrase. How could it be in the best interest of the child to ever grow up without a father? Children are born into this world with unconditional love for both parents. Why would the courts think that unlimited child support dollars is a fair trade for a child to miss out on a father's love? How can it be in the best interest of the child to grow up hating his or her father because the court failed to intervene when parental alienation was taking place? What value would these children place on marriage when they grow up after they see that getting divorced is as easy as changing your mind? If the child involved happened to be a girl, would she grow up respecting men if her mother and role model didn't? I prayed that these children wouldn't grow up valuing money over relationships, or view marriage as a vehicle to make money.

As a woman of faith, I was filled with tears when I saw how money had become society's new god. Governments were downloading the costs of raising children of divorce onto men, whether or not the children were biologically theirs, simply to save money. Many divorced women harass men to their graves for the opportunity to live life off of someone else's money. Lawyers were enticing women to go to court, with visions of riches yet to be plundered. Once in court, the lawyers were creating conflict and anger to drag things out and further fill their pockets with money. Did the judges step in to stop all this madness? Why would they? They were profiting from the misery of others, too.

I told God how I believe that every experience we have in life occurs for a reason and not by chance. We may not always understand the lesson he's trying to teach us, but as long as we have faith, we'll eventually figure it out. My godfather, who is a brilliant and insightful psychiatrist, told me that anger results from a lack of assertiveness. So as I talked to God that day, I kept asking myself where or how in my life I needed to become assertive. The more I talked, the clearer God made the lesson to me. I realized that the one constant throughout my whole conversation was the fact that every man I had known that was going through divorce had had his power taken away from him. Each one had been misunderstood and viewed as the enemy by his family, ex-wife, or the courts. No one listens to these men. Society has no tolerance for their cries of pain. They needed a voice, and I was up for the challenge. I promised God that day to make their voices heard.

CHAPTER FOURTEEN

I was about to continue with Rick's story when I heard a knock on the bedroom door. The noise startled me, causing me to abruptly shift my thoughts away from the cemetery, back into the reality of Allan's bedroom. I looked back just as Dianne came in holding two glasses of cold water. I'd gotten so engrossed in my story that I was shocked to see that nearly an hour had passed since Dianne had left the room.

"Are you two going to be much longer?" she asked.

Adam looked at me and then replied, "If you can give us another thirty minutes, then I'll come down and make dinner, I promise. Our conversation is going so well, I don't want to stop."

"No problem," Dianne said casually. "I'll just sit out back on the deck and enjoy the sunshine. Give me a holler when you come downstairs."

She'd barely left the room before Adam began bombarding me with all sorts of questions. "What happened to Tim?" he began. "Was Rick OK after the accident? How are Rick and Beth doing now?" It was nice to hear excitement in Adam's voice. He was literally sitting on the edge of the bed, leaning forward in anticipation of what I was going to say next.

"Slow down," I said with a hint of laughter in my voice. "I'll answer all your questions soon enough." I continued.

"Tim spent a total of seven days in jail for what he did. When his case went to court, the outcome amounted to nothing more than a legal slap on the wrist. Instead of being charged with attempted murder like he deserved, Tim was charged with nothing more than aggravated assault. The presiding judge sentenced him to two years less a day of community service, gave him probation, and suspended his driver's licence for three years. That's it. None of us could believe it. In court, Tim showed no remorse for what he had done, and to this day, he has never come to his father and apologized for the suffering he inflicted on this man. In fact, Beth told me that when a friend of theirs brought up the topic years later with Rick's daughter, her comment to the friend was simply, 'Oh, that,' as she laughed.

"Although Tim's sentence has long since ended, Rick and his wife continue to live out their life sentence, one of both psychological and physical pain. Even now, Rick is too traumatized to talk about what happened. Most of what I know has come from his wife. Though Rick made it out of the hospital alive and in one piece, it marked the beginning of their hell. After his release, their life became an endless stream of visits to doctors, lawyers, and court. Attempted murder didn't even satisfy his family's need to inflict pain on him. They continued to drag him back to court, looking for more money, even as they watched him being helped into court in pain and walking with a cane.

"Psychologically, the trauma left my cousin a changed man. The sense of humour that had been our bond throughout life, the emotion that Beth had fought so hard to reawaken within him following his divorce, was gone. Humour had given way to an emotional flatness, and the optimism that Beth had brought into his life had been pushed aside, replaced by negativity and sarcasm. Beth told me how they both suffered from nightmares and anxiety attacks, fearful of going beyond their own front door. Though they both went for trauma counselling, Rick began to struggle with bouts of depression and turned to pills and alcohol for comfort. His resulting downward spiral nearly ended in suicide.

"So how are they doing now? Well, it's not pretty. They lost their beautiful retirement home to legal bills and alimony payments. They live in an apartment building with high-level security because they still can't shake the anxiety attacks. They're both still so traumatized from that fateful day that they remain stuck in the past and focused on their wounds. Their apartment is full of boxes crammed with court documents and newspaper clippings, and their emotions are still as raw as the day the event occurred.

"I can only wonder that if Rick had done this to the children and it was his ex-wife complaining, would the level of legal apathy have been different? Would the authorities have removed the children from the home right away because of the emotional abuse? We'll never know, but as a woman, I can tell you that feminists lobby the government and the public tirelessly, portraying men as sexual and psychological abusers of our mothers and children. This time, the shoe was on the other foot, and everyone dropped the ball where these children were concerned. It's time that our courts and lawmakers wake up and realize that women are as capable of abusing children as men are and that the voice of every parent, whether male or female, be heard equally and given the same degree of importance when a child's safety is involved." I stopped to take a sip of water, which gave Adam a chance to jump into the conversation.

"I've got to tell you, Molly, it's nice to see someone in this day and age speak with so much conviction. With everything you've gone through, it's no wonder you're so passionate about men's rights. If you don't mind me asking, when you were in the cemetery that day after leaving the hospital, you told God that you wanted to help be the voice for divorced men who had been silenced by our system of family law. Have you thought any more about that? You've got one hell of a story to tell. If it were me, I think I'd write a book. As a man going through divorce, it would give me great comfort to know that I'm not alone. To read about other men experiencing the same emotions, struggles, and fears would help me, if only to know that I'm not fighting this uphill battle alone."

Adam's words took me back to Bill's grave once again, watching helplessly as our friendship and his body were slowly delivered back into the arms of Mother Earth. As Bill's coffin was swallowed up by the darkness, I had promised myself that he would not die in vain and that I would someday tell his story. I remember asking myself if he had chosen to die or if it had simply been his time. I'd never know.

And who would tell my cousin's story?

It's a sad reflection on today's society that divorce has become an accepted way of life. Just as we've become desensitized to watching sex or violence on television, we have detached ourselves from the emotional impact that this process has on men. When another man loses his home, his money, and, often, his children, there is no mention of it in the media, no public outcry. No concerts are rushed into production around the world to raise money and awareness for this man's plight. No, divorced men are often forgotten. They often must depend on the kindness of friends or family for a bed to sleep in or a hot meal.

What if this same man falls down on his luck and loses his job? Will society prop him up until he gets back on his feet? He may be eligible for welfare or unemployment insurance, but once the government garnishes child-support and spousal payments, he'll be left with little to live on. Imagine the anguish a loving father feels sitting in a jail cell, his only crime being that he lost his job or declared bankruptcy. He didn't refuse to pay his support, he just couldn't.

How is this different from throwing a decent father and husband in jail for not being able to make his house or car payments? Would his family stand by and let this happen? Would society get away with this? I don't think so. Both cases involve men who want to do the right thing but can't, for reasons beyond their own control.

Why is justice being dispensed so harshly in one instance but not the other? And then it hit me: The key here is *awareness*. People can't fix a problem they aren't aware of. And what better way to get awareness on a large scale than by writing a book? I began to get excited.

"You know what, Adam?" I said excitedly. "I've thought about it, and you're right. I'm going to write a book about my experiences. If I do my job right, the reader will walk away with awareness of the problems and a desire to help seek change. Society needs to be knocked off its complacent pedestal and realize that real people with shattered lives provide the fuel behind our divorce statistics. It's the person who turns a blind eye to the problem and the suffering of others who will cry the loudest when he becomes the next victim of divorce. The beauty is that with awareness comes the opportunity for open dialogue and positive change.

"In my opinion, the general public, aided by the feminists, has bought into a negative stereotype of divorced men, viewing their anger as unwarranted, fabricated, and somewhat over the top. Many of my married friends say, 'It can't be that bad, or we would have heard about it in the media.' I get frustrated because I know that it's not hard to spin the truth. I've been interviewed in the past and have seen my own words and views twisted against me in print. The stories are there, but they are overshadowed by society's perception that when it comes to divorce, the women and the children are to be viewed as the victims while the man is to be viewed as someone who is simply crying foul as a means to escape financial obligations.

"Changing the public's perception won't be easy. I'm only one person, but I have a big dream. I want to do this, not only for Bill's memory, but also for my cousin, for you, and for all the other men and women who are being unfairly punished. I'm not anti-women or pro-men. I just happen to be someone who has seen too much of the dirty side of the divorce game, and I've got to call it as I see it. If people read my words and judge me as taking one side over the other, that's their opinion, and I can't change that. The only side I intend to take is the side of truth. In my experience, it's always been people with the most to lose who cry out the loudest when the truth is revealed. My godfather said it even better: 'None proclaim their innocence as loud as the guilty.' You know, Adam, I just realized that I've been monopolizing the conversation. I think it's time that you get a chance to talk. I really don't know anything about you. I don't even know how you ended up in this house."

"Are you sure you want to hear my story? You must be getting hungry." Just as at Dianne's house a week earlier, Adam was again trying to deflect the conversation away from him, but this time I wasn't buying it.

"I want to hear your story," I said. I sat quietly for a moment, waiting for him to begin, and then I followed my last comment up with a simple "please."

Adam began to talk.

"When I was a little boy, I grew up in a very dysfunctional home. My mother was an alcoholic and was often mentally unstable. My father was present in body but was not emotionally available to his kids. I felt invisible within my parents' world. I spent a lot of my time playing alone, always wondering what I needed to do in order to get their attention, feel valued, and, most importantly, feel loved.

"When I became a teenager, my home life didn't improve; in fact, it got worse. My parents went through an ugly and often violent divorce. I began focusing my attention on school so that I didn't have to think about the pain I was feeling inside. I knew that if I got high marks, the academic doors would fly open. Then I could finally run away from my dysfunctional past and start a new life, one of my own choosing and that I had control over.

"In total, I spent ten years in university before graduating as a dentist. I paid for all of my education myself by getting student loans and working at multiple part-time jobs, often at the same time. It was worth it. When I graduated, I felt a deep sense of accomplishment and truly believed that with my newfound education, the worst of my life was behind me.

"After a few years in practice, I was ready to meet someone nice, start a family, and settle down. I was determined not to follow in my parents' footsteps. I was going to tread carefully, because one messy divorce in my lifetime was more than enough. When I met and then eventually married my wife, she decided early on in the marriage that she wanted to further her education. Like any loving husband would, I paid for everything so that she could also become a professional in her chosen path.

It was a real struggle for me financially, but I didn't complain, because our marriage was for life, right?

"Everything went smoothly in the relationship until our son, Allan, was born. After that, it was like a switch went off in my wife's head. Her only priority became Allan, and just like in my childhood, I became invisible once again. We no longer had any emotional connection to one another. I ceased to be of any value to her except for what I could provide financially for the family. That never changed for the rest of the marriage. Even at the end when I knew in my heart that our marriage was dead, I still tried to save it by going for marriage counselling, mainly for Allan's sake. I was willing to do anything, even forgo my own happiness, as long as it ensured that I would always be part of that little boy's life.

"Well, we both know how that all turned out. So here I sit. Now, about this house...

CHAPTER FIFTEEN

"I bought this house because I didn't want to raise my son in a tiny apartment with no backyard to play in. I spent money from my line of credit to buy him furniture and toys that I really couldn't afford. I was desperate to create a true "home" environment for my son, because love overrules logic when you want your child back. I even made sure that this house was close to his school so he could keep the same friends and I could walk him to school, since he would be living with me fifty percent of the time. Even my lawyer was buying into the fifty-fifty custody arrangement as a viable option. In my mind, it was a no-brainer; I was a great father to my son and loved him unconditionally. My lawyer was going to bat for me, and my commitment to my child's upbringing was equal to his mother's. What could possibly go wrong?

"In hindsight, my downfall was that I believed the legal system was actually fair and that my lawyer honestly cared about the outcome of my case. After waiting nearly seven months from the time I first got separated, I was finally going to get my day in court and have this custody and access issue behind me. I was scared but excited at the same time. My deal on this house was about to close, and I was looking forward to having my son with me every other week, or two weeks at a time–those details didn't matter; they could be worked out later. The important thing was that I had followed my lawyer's advice to the letter and now felt confident that I was finally going to start a new life with my little boy at my side.

"I've got to tell you, Molly, those seven months leading up to that day in court were a living hell. My lawyer had told me that until some sort of custody arrangement was worked out, I should plan on living in the matrimonial home with my ex-wife. The reason for this, she said, was that if I left early, no matter how tense the living arrangement was, I would be sending a message to the court that my ex-wife was the better parent. She also advised me that if I moved out too early, not only might the court view this action as abandonment of the child on my part, but it would also give my ex-wife the right to change the locks and keep me out, legally. Once you pack up your bags and walk out that door, you give up all rights to your own home, even though you're often still paying the mortgage and all the bills.

"So I did what any father who loves his child would do. Against my better judgement, I stayed. I endured seven months of "living" in the spare bedroom and eating every meal alone in the basement. If that wasn't bad enough, I had to watch my ex-wife monopolize my son's time to the point where I couldn't get a moment alone with him. Then she would accuse me of being a poor excuse for a father because I wasn't spending enough time with him. The only time she acknowledged my presence was as she was casting me a hateful glance, threatening me with legal action if we couldn't agree on something, or was busy scribbling down detailed notes on my every move. I learned later that note-taking is a common practice amongst spouses and is often initiated by their lawyers. If a woman was married to a good husband and father, she has to dig deep and use every tool, including false accusations, in order to discredit him as an unfit father.

"For the most part, my ex and I didn't talk for those seven months. If she was talking to Allan and I added a comment, she wouldn't acknowledge my presence. In her mind I was simply the ghost that came home every night, left every morning, and paid all the bills. I was willing to put up with all the abuse because I believed my lawyer. If I could make it to that custody hearing, I'd end this nightmare and start a new home life with my son, free of watchful eyes.

"When the big day came, I was barely in my court seat before the presiding judge sat down and announced that my son would reside the majority of the time with my ex-wife. Her view was that a young child "may" need a father in their life but "definitely" needs a mother. It made no difference that, like his mother, I loved my son and had been an integral part of his life every day. My heart sank. I felt like I'd been kicked in the stomach. I wanted to scream, but I had to sit there and quietly accept my ruling. There was no rebuttal or objection from my lawyer. All I got for the four hundred dollars an hour I was spending was a polite "thank-you, your Honour," and then it was over. How could the judge make such an important decision in both my child's life and mine without first listening to arguments from both sides?

"After court ended, I waited in the stairwell for my lawyer. I wanted to talk to her privately. I needed answers. Waiting on a stair step, I broke down and cried. The pain of the last seven months reverberated off the walls as I wept. I was incapable of controlling my emotions, even as people walked past and whispered under their breaths. When my lawyer came through the door, I jumped to my feet and yelled, "What the hell happened in there? In your office, you made it sound like shared equal custody would be a shoe-in for me, yet you didn't say anything on my behalf in court. You just sat there and did nothing!" She then had the nerve to begin talking to me in an apathetic and condescending voice following the worst loss of my life. The court was taking my son away from me–my only child! My lawyer said there was nothing she could do for me and that the judge had already made up her mind.

"I hadn't been allowed to voice my opinions or objections in the courtroom that day. I had left that job to my lawyer, and she'd failed me miserably. Somewhere in the middle of that pep talk she had given me in her office about how I had a good chance of getting equal living time with my son, she'd somehow neglected to tell me how the courts award mother's custody of the children nearly eighty-five percent of the time.

"I was angry with my lawyer–not so much with her attitude as with the fact that she knew I was very upset and emotional where my son was concerned. In my opinion, she took advantage of my fragile state and gave me false hope concerning the outcome of my hearing. Telling me that my expectations were not realistic within the current court system would have allowed me to decide if this was something I still wanted to fight for, and at what financial cost. False hope did nothing more for me than simply pad an already bloated legal bill.

"When it was all said and done, I'd have been better off to have followed my gut instinct and moved out of the house as soon as I got separated. If someone had told me outright just how bad the custody odds are stacked against men in court, I would never have bought this house believing I'd have my son. I would never have gotten lawyers involved like I did, either. As it stands now, I only see my son one evening a week and every other weekend. I'm told it's the gold standard for most fathers as far as child access is concerned. I didn't need a high-priced lawyer to figure that schedule out.

"If I had been smarter, I would have rented an apartment, given my ex what she wants, within reason, and just moved on with my life. You won't change a judge's opinion on child custody, and everything else is just stuff. It's not worth losing your health or putting yourself into an early grave fighting over something as small as a kettle or even as large as a house. Look at me. You don't know me that well, but I'll tell you, this divorce has aged me twenty years. I'm on the verge of going bankrupt, and I'm saddled with a mortgage I can't afford. I was so stupid to let my emotions get the best of me. I bought into the lawyer's 'fight at any cost' mentality. Instead of filling up my child's education fund for the future, I put all my hard-earned money into lining lawyer's pockets."

After hearing his story, I said, "I understand why you bought this house, Adam, and that you didn't get the access schedule you'd hoped for, but I still don't understand why this bedroom isn't being used. I mean, you should have your son at least every other weekend, right?"

"You're absolutely right. But after hearing your cousin's story and how his ex-wife alienated his children against him, I think that's what happened to me; I just didn't have a name for what I was going through at the time. After getting divorced, I understood that both my ex and I would want to spend as much time with Allan as possible. Who wouldn't? That's normal, but what disturbed me was that I felt like I was being methodically pushed out of my child's life, and for no good reason.

"In my case, my support payments are so high because of my profession that, after paying the mortgage, grocery, house, and lawyer bills, I had no money left to spend on my son when he came to visit. He didn't understand why we couldn't go places or even out for a pizza. We played games together, read books, went for walks, or watched television, but that was it.

"At the other end was my ex-wife with all my money, and believe me, she made the most of it. My son told me on numerous occasions how much fun it was living at Mom's house. Anything Allan wanted, he got. The weekends were always planned around pleasing him and making every moment special. With all the outings to restaurants, birthday parties, toy stores, and lessons of every imaginable type, Allan was never given the opportunity to be bored. Personally, I think being bored sometimes is important because it makes kids become creative, and they learn to entertain themselves.

"I knew that I couldn't compete with all the activities at his mother's house, nor did I want to. Still, it was frustrating to think that my income was being used to help make his mother look like the fun parent of the family. After a while, you get sick and tired of hearing how great it is at Mom's house or about where they went on the weekend at your expense. My ex never even bothered to explain to my son that I was giving her money each month so that they could do all those activities, effectively making me look like the cheap parent or the one who wasn't willing to part with his money. She seemed like some type of hero, looking like the parent who was willing to sacrifice everything just to make him happy.

"Over time, my ex-wife started planning events for Allan on my time, which went against our divorce agreement. This would include out-of-town weekend hockey tournaments in the winter or baseball tournaments in the summer. She knew that I couldn't afford the hotel and food costs, so she would offer to take Allan on my behalf. I was in a no-win situation. If I kept Allan because it was our weekend together, he'd miss the tournament and I would come off looking like the bad parent. If I let him go, then his mother would come off looking like the hero. Once again, she was there to save the day when I couldn't. Eventually, a large chunk of my one-on-one time with Allan eroded away to nothing as more and more events got planned for him on my weeknight and weekends. My objections fell on deaf ears, as my ex knew that I didn't have the money to take her back to court and enforce the divorce agreement we had both signed.

"She got involved in every aspect of our son's life, from school committees and volunteering to coaching for any sport he was part of. She even asked to help at every birthday party he was invited to. There was nowhere I could go with my son and be alone.

"As time went by, I began to notice a definite change in my son's attitude. When he was at my house, he would begin reminding me an hour before I had to take him home that we had to leave soon. He would always ask me what events I had planned for him, as he was never able to sit quietly and entertain himself. He started becoming quite snippy with me, commenting on everything from his level of boredom to the quality of the meals I was serving him. His words and his body language made it clear to me that he viewed Mom's house as fun and Dad's house as boring.

"In our divorce agreement, there was a clause which stated that Allan would have the final say as to whether he had to do something or not. I know that was stupid, but if I hadn't agreed to it, I'd still be battling with my ex-wife's lawyer today. My ex used that clause to her advantage, reinforcing to Allan that he didn't have to come to my house if he didn't want to, and not to feel guilty about his decision. Eventually, Allan started phoning me himself. I could hear my ex in the background feeding him lines, as he once again explained why he couldn't spend time with me. After a while, I stopped hearing the excuses. Why fight it? I knew in my heart that the alienation, as you call it, was complete.

"So there you have it. I'm left with a bedroom decorated for a king but inhabited by ghosts. I miss him, Molly, but what can I do? I mean, what could your cousin have done differently? I have no control over this situation. This isn't the hill I'm going to die on. Thanks to you, I now realize that I have to let it go and move on with my life. If I don't, it will eat me up and make me sick. If my ex wants to be hurtful, or if Allan doesn't want to be here, that's their choice. The one thing I do have control over is how I choose to react to the situation.

"I see by my watch that there's one more thing I have control over, and that's when we eat. I promised Dianne that we'd be down in thirty minutes and it's already been an hour. I'd better get downstairs and get the barbeque started. You must be getting hungry, and Dianne is going to start spreading rumours if we stay up here talking any longer." We headed downstairs to find Dianne and start supper.

"I guess we didn't need to worry about Dianne," I said to Adam, loud enough that Dianne could hear.

"I heard that, Molly Murphy," Dianne snapped back sarcastically, popping out from behind the open refrigerator door with three cold beers in hand. "You're lucky you have a friend like me who thinks ahead. I heard you guys coming down the stairs, and I thought you might be thirsty since you were up there talking for an hour." She made sure to emphasize the word 'hour' but gave me a playful wink at the same time, letting me know that she was just having fun with Adam. He was about to start apologizing when Dianne flashed him a grin to let him know that she was just kidding.

"Look, ladies," Adam said, "why don't you take your beers and relax in the living room? There's nothing I need help with. I'll call you when dinner's ready." Before we could say anything, he was already headed towards the backdoor, hamburgers in hand.

As I sat in the living room, chatting with Dianne, I got up and wandered over to the fireplace. I looked once again at the photographs that Adam had shown me when we first arrived. I now knew what he meant when he had said that divorce had aged him twenty years. In these pictures, his eyes sparkled with joy, his face was full of colour, and he radiated health. The pictures had obviously been taken during happier times.

Divorce could never touch the essence of who he is, but the Adam I had just sat and talked with upstairs looked tired and worn down by life. He was pale in comparison to those old pictures, and he'd lost a lot of weight. His eyes looked hollow and lifeless. The youthfulness in those photographs was gone. Now the stress of divorce was etching its way onto his face and into his life.

The pictures of Adam were no different than those I had seen hanging on the walls in Rick's house, or Bill's, for that matter–happy men, proud fathers and husbands, blissfully unaware of the hell they would eventually endure at the hands of their spouse. If someone could have warned them of what lay ahead, maybe they could have done things differently or at least prepared better.

It's no different than looking at an old picture of someone you know who contracts terminal cancer. Wouldn't you have told them to enjoy life, focus on family and not work, if you knew where their life was headed before they did?

I was beginning to see divorce in the same light. Giving men the heads-up before disaster strikes would be the key. There are various scenarios that tend to play themselves out with predictable results, thanks to gender bias in the courts and past performance where family law is concerned. In reading about the experiences and emotions of people like Adam, foresight would be available to individuals going through divorce.

For example, a man could know ahead of time if he decides to fight a particular legal battle or react in a certain way what the probable outcome would be. This information would be priceless. Women already have money and the courts on their side, so men need knowledge on theirs, or their battles will be lost before they even begin. What a powerful way, I thought, for men like Adam, Rick, and Bill to turn a negative experience like divorce into something positive for all those men who are unfortunate enough to be following in their footsteps.

When Adam gave us the call for dinner, I quickly headed for the table. I was really hungry, but not for food. I was hungry for knowledge. I now had a book to write and men to fight for. Adam didn't know it yet, but our conversation over dinner would be much more than idle chat. This would be a dinner none of us would ever forget.

CHAPTER SIXTEEN

Out back, my senses were greeted by the smell of homemade burgers. Through the barbeque smoke, I could see contentment on Adam's face as he tended to the grill. Dianne and I sat at the table, sipped freshly poured red wine, and waited for him. The sun was beginning to set behind the trees as Adam turned off the barbeque and joined us. He sat down across from me, beaming with pride at his stack of burgers. We said grace and then toasted to our friendship.

I waited until we were done eating before reopening our discussion about divorce. A symphony of crickets pierced the night air as we took turns telling stories and having a few good belly laughs. I watched Adam whenever he was talking and knew that he felt happy and safe, like those photographs on the fireplace mantle. As wounded and hurting as he was, I have to admit that there was something captivating about him. I was beginning to feel protective of him, in that I didn't want to let anyone else hurt him. I felt that, surrounded by good friends who would never judge him, Adam would be more willing to open up to me again. As he reached across the table to refill my wine glass, I took the opportunity to ask him another question.

"Of all the things you've gone through during your divorce, what would you say is the hardest thing you've had to deal with?"

As soon as those words left my lips, I sensed an awkward silence, like I'd somehow overstepped my bounds. He finished pouring my wine, sat down, and began fidgeting with the salt and pepper-shakers in front of him. He wouldn't look at me. I knew that my question had unnerved him, but I sensed that he wanted to open up. He was struggling to find the words, so I sat and waited. Then it happened, the moment I had waited all evening for. He looked up at me, misty-eyed, and began to talk. Once that floodgate opened, there was no turning back. He then gave me one of the best lessons in what it's like to be a man going through divorce that I would ever hear.

"You don't understand, Molly. I can't pick just one thing that's the hardest to deal with. For any man going through divorce, every day is a matter of survival. You're in the middle of a nightmare that you have no control over. One day you have a wife, children, and financial security. Then, in the blink of an eye, it's all gone. You're no longer a husband, and the courts effectively strip you of your ability to be a father to your children. You struggle to find meaning in your life. Everything you cherish and have ever worked for is taken from you.

"Your friends who have never gone through divorce do their best to comfort you, by patting you on the back, telling you things will get better or to just get on with your life. But it's not that easy. They have no understanding of the pain and struggles you're going through. It's not their fault. How can you expect them to understand the emptiness a man feels in the pit of his stomach as he drops his house keys in a mailbox and walks away from the only life he's ever known as if it never existed?

"Only a divorced man can understand what it feels like to be rejected by his own family and then be thrown to the curb like a worthless old couch, to be relegated to the status of a paycheque without a face, where you are only valued for what others can take from you, not for who you are as a person. Night-time is the hardest for me. I cry myself to sleep each night, but only God hears me, because I'm alone. I tell myself maybe this time when I close my eyes and pull the covers up over my head, it will all go away, maybe tomorrow will be the day that I wake up and realize that it was all a dream. But the nightmare never ends.

"I don't know if I'll survive this. I'm not trying to be pessimistic, just honest. I'm tired and just want it to stop. I rarely see my son anymore. No matter how this all plays out, I will never stop carrying that feeling of hope that someday, when Allan's older, he'll realize how much I fought for him. I need something to believe in, something that I can cling to. When things look really dark and that trapped feeling begins to overwhelm me, I get scared because my thoughts turn to suicide. I bet a lot of men think of suicide.

"I used to be judgemental and often viewed people who took their own lives as selfish or cowardly. Not anymore. Until you've walked a mile in someone else's shoes, you can never understand what they have gone through. I'm not a weak person, but there are moments when I'm overcome with anxiety and panic. You feel yourself sinking deeper into the quicksand, with no one there trying to pull you out. I wake up wondering who'll be demanding their pound of flesh today. Will it be a creditor, my ex-wife, or maybe her lawyer? Perhaps it will be my own lawyers when they realize I can't pay. Don't get me wrong, I don't believe that suicide is ever the answer; a person shouldn't have to die in order to have inner peace.

"How can a man find inner peace and the will to continue? There's no easy answer to that question. What could I possibly say to a father who doesn't get to see his children? Or a man who has gone bankrupt or lost his job but is still expected to make full support payments or face losing his licence and passport and doing possible jail time? Then, if he manages to get a new job, the Family Responsibility Office rushes in, garnishes his wages for back payment of support, and again leaves him poverty-stricken and defeated. It's a wonder people are shocked when the headlines tell us of another divorced man taking his life. What do we expect when you take away a man's dignity and sense of self-worth?

"Divorced men have been put in a bad position. If they become vocal over the inequalities they face, some feminists label them as hostile and bitter. Their only other option is to stay silent and simply accept that these inequalities exist. The true path to change rarely follows the easiest route; just ask the African- Americans who were forced to sit at the back of the bus not even sixty years ago. What's the difference between the discrimination these people faced and the discrimination divorced men face today? Why are the African-Americans, who rose up and spoke out for change in the Sixties, viewed as trailblazers, but divorced men doing the same thing viewed as bitter?

"I don't understand our legal system, either. It doesn't tolerate wife or child abuse, but what about the abuse I'm going through right now? Why doesn't the destruction of my life matter to anyone? My pain and suffering isn't even a blip on the radar to politicians and lawmakers. We've moved ahead by leaps and bounds when it comes to the rights of minorities, gays, and lesbians, but what about the rights of divorced men? I feel like I'm living back in the time of slavery, where an African-American was considered to be only two-thirds of a person. Now it's the divorced male who has taken on this status. They had civil rights leaders fighting for their cause; who will be the voice for us?

"I know that I'm talking about a lot of different things, but it's because I am so frustrated inside. Right now, what I need and what would make me happiest would be for my ex-wife and her lawyer to simply go away and leave me in peace. All I've ever asked for from life is to be loved, to give love, and to raise a family, but they won't let me get on with my life. I would never kick a man when he's down, but that's what our divorce laws let women do. It's nothing less than legalized harassment.

"I remember as a child seeing some older boys torturing a rabbit they had trapped in the corner of a neighbour's garage. I screamed at them to stop, but they just laughed and ignored me. They poked it with a sharp stick until it died, and even then, kept poking at it just for fun. They finally left with no remorse for what they'd done. Sometimes I feel like that rabbit, and it's my ex and her lawyer who are holding the stick. I have nothing left for them to take, but they just keep poking at me. They don't have to worry about me dying, either, because I'm already there inside. That happened the moment I lost my son.

"I now live in a constant state of fear and anxiety, afraid to go to my mail-box in case there's another letter from my ex-wife's lawyer demanding that I give her more money. If it's not money they're after, it's my reputation. At last count, I think I'm up to over one hundred accusations put forth against me attempting to prove that I'm an unfit father. Apparently, I never knew how bad a person or unfit a father I was until her lawyer explained it all to me in writing.

"I'm learning quickly that when it comes to divorce, the man is guilty until he proves himself innocent. My ex-wife is allowed to accuse me of anything she can dream up, yet the onus is on me to prove my innocence in a court of law. If I don't, I'll be presumed guilty, so my legal bills continue to skyrocket and put me that much closer to going bankrupt. Every time my lawyer proves her accusations false, two things happen: my mailbox fills up with new accusations and my lawyer sends me another bill I can't pay.

"The courts promote this ongoing harassment by providing a forum to present each accusation, no matter how petty or absurd. After all, it isn't the judge or lawyer's problem if I'm going broke. To make matters worse, each time an accusation gets dismissed, the judge simply moves on to the next one, without my ex receiving so much as a slap on the wrist for the horrific stress and financial burden she has subjected me to. When I tell my lawyer that I've had enough of these false accusations and that I want this runaway financial train to stop, her answer is simple: "Give her everything, or fight–those are your two options." Either way, you can't stop the financial bloodletting.

"Believe me, when you are a professional and run your own business, both the bloodletting and the harassment get turned up a notch. Your life is under a microscope. Not only has every aspect of my personal life been invaded through legal letters, phone calls, and e-mails, but now, every purchase, transaction, and decision I make concerning my business is scrutinized by my ex-wife and her lawyer as they look for one more penny to pilfer. I'm constantly on the defensive, being made to explain my actions, though I've done nothing wrong. I'm made to feel like a criminal, a liar, or both.

"If I forget to give them one document they've asked for or I say that I can't find it, it's automatically assumed that I'm hiding something. That's when letters threatening court action begin to appear, and once again, my lawyer gets involved. Every time I give them financial documentation, I end up spending costly time with my accountant. Then they turn around and ask for more, like it's a game to them. My lawyer says that I'm obligated to give them whatever they ask for, no matter what the financial cost is to me. She knows that they're trying to financially drown me, but there's nothing that can be done to stop it. I feel like I'm losing my mind.

"My once profitable business, which I built from the ground up, is collapsing around me like a deck of cards because I can't think straight. I'm not making rational business decisions or focusing on my patients' needs because the threat of court action is always in the back of my mind. I'm wasting my valuable time gathering documentation to hand over to my ex-wife's lawyer. Then I have to watch as the information is twisted out of context and used in court to bury me. It's like handing bullets to the firing squad or bringing my own rope to my hanging.

"I'm barely making enough to keep my doors open, yet I still have to make support payments based on a level of income that no longer exists. My staff members get paid while most weeks I go home empty handed. The odd week that I do get a paycheque, it's enough to cover my mortgage but not enough to buy groceries and pay the bills. I make too much money to qualify for legal aid, yet I'm paying so much in support that I can't afford a lawyer to try and get my payments lowered. I'm afraid that if I take my ex-wife back to court over the support issue, I'll lose and be forced to pay her court costs. I know of what I speak, because it's already happened."

CHAPTER SEVENTEEN

"When I first went to court to determine what my spousal support obligations would be, the judge ruled that I was responsible for paying my ex-wife's court costs of more than three thousand dollars. The logic was that even though the judge eventually awarded her thousands less than she was asking for, my lawyer had offered one hundred dollars less than what the judge felt was an adequate compensation, so I got stuck with her bill.

"As bad as it was being stuck with that bill, it pales in comparison to listening to her lawyer rationalize why her client should be awarded so much of my money. The argument was that her client should be compensated for having gone from a full-time position down to a part-time one to help with the child-rearing responsibility of our son. At that time, I had the larger income and worked longer hours, so it made good financial sense that I be the one working full time. We would save on day-care costs, and I was happy knowing that our son would be home the majority of the time, getting lots of love and attention.

"I still remember the joyful look on my wife's face at the prospect of staying home. She had originally brought this idea to me and had looked into working part time before we started talking about doing this. I kept asking her if this is what she really wanted to do, and she kept saying yes. She had even sat me down and gone over the numbers with me. She'd already found that the savings in day-care costs, coupled with her pay, would lose us very little financially. She told me that she'd enjoy staying at home, as it would give her time to really experience being a mother for the first time.

"By the time we got to court, that scenario had drastically changed. When my ex-wife's lawyer stood up in front of the judge and started talking, I looked around to see whom she was talking about. Then I realized it was me! She portrayed me as a self-centred, cold-hearted individual who put his business interests ahead of family. She portrayed my ex-wife as the self-sacrificing victim who had given up career opportunities and income to raise her child while giving her husband time to further his career. I stared at her lawyer in amazement. This was all new to me.

"After hearing all of this, I honestly believed her argument would go nowhere. I mean, when you get married, you work as a team, right? You do what's best for your family, and you sacrifice. To me, raising a child can't be reduced to some sort of business transaction. It's a natural integrated part of the whole marriage package. Unfortunately for me, the judge decided that her argument had merit. I watched, dumbfounded, as once again, I came out on the short end of the stick. I was forced to cough up more of my hard-earned income, which I couldn't afford to lose, for support. I was giving my ex more money each month, on top of her income, than I took home.

"My lawyer explained that if your wife stays home with your child, even just part time, while you go back to work, the court calculates the amount of income she gave up, had she still been working her normal full-time hours. The court also takes into consideration income she "may" have lost out on because of not being able to accept an advancement or new job while at home with a child. That potential income gets factored into their calculations. As a man, you have two choices when you and your wife have a baby together: You can tell her to go back to work full-time right away so that she doesn't lose any income, making you look like an insensitive husband, or you can let her stay home, and pray you never get divorced. I'll never forget my lawyer's parting words to me that day: "If you get married, stay married, and if you're not married, don't."

"Things are so tight that I've been dishing out support payments by using my line of credit, credit cards, and money I had set aside to pay my taxes. I'm a dentist of almost twenty years and counting my pennies every week so that I can eat while handing over thousands each month to my ex-wife, who has a full-time job and lives in a beautiful home I helped to pay for. It's gut-wrenching when you know your future is headed for disaster and all you can do is wait for the inevitable. I can't think of a worse fate than being absolutely powerless over your destiny and knowing that the ability to make decisions for yourself is no longer an option.

"I even went back to see my lawyer when I'd reached my emotional and financial breaking point. I figured that once she looked at how much support I was paying out versus what I was bringing in, she'd find some way to help me. I was wrong. Her chief concern was not my future welfare, but how I was going to pay her. Her way of helping me was to have me sign some document ensuring that when the divorce was all said and done, she'd get paid first from any proceeds and I'd get what might be remaining. Her only legal advice that day was to refer me to a junior lawyer within the same firm for help, because their hourly rate was cheaper.

"When I retold my story to the junior lawyer, she said that I would have to file a motion in court to get my support payments lowered but that it would cost three thousand dollars, which I didn't have. She, too, could see from my financial statements that I was nearly bankrupt but told me to try and hang on, borrow money from family or friends to pay my ex, and hope that when our final court date arrived, the judge would lower my payments. Unfortunately, hope is a rare commodity when you are a man going through divorce.

"Like I said earlier, society acts so surprised when another divorced man takes his own life. After all, it's our own laws that are driving men to this extreme. When I was ten years old, my brother's hockey coach, who was also a neighbour, took his own life. At the time, I wondered about what could be so bad in someone's life that they would want to end it. Now, after seeing that junior lawyer and wondering if I had enough money to put gas in my car to get home, I don't wonder as much. I really believe that if something doesn't change soon for divorced men, we're going to bury a lot more good fathers in the future. If it weren't for good friends and my strong faith in God, I'd be a statistic by now.

"I could talk all night about the injustice of divorce, but what's the point? Don't get me wrong, I love talking to you, Molly, but with you, I'm already preaching to the converted. You know firsthand how bad it is out there for men, but it's the general public that needs a wake-up call. The attitude out there is "out of sight, out of mind. As long as it doesn't affect me personally, then I don't have to think about it." Well, I'll tell you, anyone who thinks they are immune to the ravages of divorce is naive, stupid, or both. With half of all marriages ending in divorce, there's hardly anyone left on the planet that hasn't gone through it or doesn't know someone who has. No man should ever be so arrogant as to think that his marriage is divorce-proof. The next-door neighbour, the one with the perfect marriage and the smiling wife, probably thought the same thing, too, right up until the moment he handed her his life savings in a lawyer's office.

"It's hard for us to understand how people living in a country halfway around the world can kill each other in the name of religion or how millions of people can die of starvation each year when we have so much, but that doesn't change the fact that it's happening. The easiest solution to any problem that we don't want to deal with is feigning ignorance of its existence. Once you convince people that a problem doesn't exist, then society has no obligation to deal with it. Global warming is one good example–the global decimation of men's rights is another.

"Anyone can be made to believe anything if they hear it enough times. Take Hitler, for example. He was able to change the belief system of a complete nation with nothing more than the power of the spoken word. I admit, when I was first married, I to fell victim to its power. I remember sitting down with a good friend of mine over a beer while he poured his heart out to me over his divorce. What he told me seemed so hard to believe that I was left thinking that he must be stretching the truth or lying. It couldn't be that one-sided in a democratic country like Canada, I thought.

"The problem is, he wasn't lying, because now I'm going through what he did. The real problem back then was my own ignorance, because I chose to believe a false truth rather than believing in the words of a lifelong friend. He had no reason to lie to me. What would he have to gain? Can we say the same thing of our politicians and feminists?

"When I think back to that conversation, I'm ashamed for ever doubting my friend's word. Now that I'm walking in his shoes, I understand how important it is to be heard. When I got divorced, I fell into a deep depression. I tried to reach out to my family for support, but my words were met with nothing deeper than "that's too bad" or a resounding "really?" If my own flesh and blood won't acknowledge the pain I'm going through, how could I ever expect society to embrace my plight?

"My life as I once knew it has been stripped away. The sweet sound of my child's laughter or the clinking of cutlery at a family meal has been replaced by silence. When a loving but boisterous family surrounds you, those moments of silence are a welcome respite. Not now. The feelings of isolation and lon liness follow me like a shadow. There is no escape from the emptiness I feel within my soul. When people talk of heaven and hell, I look forward to heaven, because I'm living in hell.

"When I look down the road at where my life is headed, I don't see a future–I see a life sentence. Once my business is bankrupt, I won't be able to get a loan, have a credit card, or even rent an apartment without a co-signer. All my patients will be gone, but not before reading the bankruptcy signs adorning my business windows. I'm sure that my demise will be the topic of conversation around many dinner tables.

"And at almost fifty, if I ever want to practice again, I'll have to put my pride in check and beg some young new dentist for a job. It will be begging, because there's nothing else I'm trained to do. I'll be forced to start a new patient base from scratch because family law says that I have to keep supporting the lifestyle that my ex-wife became accustomed to during our marriage. I just have to laugh at it all, or else I will cry. My ex gets to have a "lifestyle" while I don't even get to have a life. If I work night and day, the best I could hope for is to make enough money to keep me out of arrears with my support payments. While the friends I went to dental school with are dreaming about retirement and the trips they'll go on, I'll just be grateful to have a roof over my head and food in the fridge. My reality is that I'll work until I die, because I have to eat. I worked hard for what I achieved in life, and now it's gone.

"When I first got married, I thought I knew what love was, but what I really learned is what it isn't. Any woman who can take a man's last dime and then come back looking for more does not have the capacity to love anyone except herself. I believe in God, and I believe we all stand before God when we die and are judged for how our actions in life affected other people. Is there a God? Who knows, but if I'm right, I hope that all these women are made to feel the pain they put their husbands and their children through, who, more often than not, were denied, against their will, the love of their fathers.

"I don't hate women. In fact, my dream would be to grow old with someone who truly loves me, but who is going to want me down the road? I'll have nothing left of any value to offer anybody. I'll be a bankrupt, baggage-ridden, and nearly fifty-year-old man with no hope of financial recovery. I won't be able to support myself, let alone support a new family. What would I say if I did somehow get married again and my new wife had kids of her own? "Hey kids, I'd love to provide for you, but I have to give all my money to my ex-wife so that my son can have everything he wants while you get nothing. Don't ask me for anything, because I can't give it to you. Also, try not to get upset when Allan flaunts everything he has in front of you. You are special to me and I do love you, but you just have to accept being second best." I don't think so! I'll spend the rest of my life alone, and even die alone if I have to, before I'll allow anyone else to get hurt because of my life choices. I've said enough. I can't talk about it any-more."

"I'm proud of you, Adam. Hold your head up high. You are a courageous man, and don't let anyone ever tell you differently. Whenever I would get down, my mother would always say, 'God never makes junk. You are perfect.' And you are perfect, Adam. Remember, you are much more than what people see. Your words tonight are going to help comfort many men and inspire change, because no one will read your words and not be moved. Your voice, along with Bill and Rick's, will be heard, because it's my time to talk now. It's time for me to help carry the flag for your cause. My time standing on the sidelines is over. My sword will be my pen, my shield will be the truth, and with every word I write, I'll gain both strength and courage from the thousands of divorced men who stand behind me in spirit. They'll be thankful that their collective voices are being heard and that a female has finally said, 'Enough!'"

CHAPTER EIGHTEEN

Leaving Adam's that night, I felt so bad for him. I drove away as he stood on the porch, waving good-bye. Why would anyone want to hurt such a kind and gentle man? I could tell he didn't want me to leave, that he wasn't ready to go back in the house and face his loneliness once again. He reminded me of a child being left at school for the first time. They look at you with a mixture of puzzlement and fear, as if they are saying, "Please don't leave me. I'm scared. When are you coming back?" All without the need for words.

I waited until Adam was safely inside before driving away. Tomorrow morning, I knew, I'd wake up to the laughter and smiles of my three beautiful daughters. I wouldn't be able to get a word in edge-wise as they playfully argue back and forth at the kitchen table. What will Adam do? Wake up tired from yet another tearful night and spend another day alone, without his son. I'm proud of his courage and his strength. I don't know how he does it. My girls are my whole life; the thought of not having them with me makes me feel sick.

When I really stopped to think about it, I realized it wasn't the legal system that took all of Adam's money or alienated him from his child. I put the blame solely on the shoulders of his ex-wife. Women who can do this have made a conscious decision to hurt their former spouses. The legal system lays out the template of how to destroy men, but it's the women's choice to pull the trigger.

I was too wound up to head straight home to bed. I've always had the habit of going for a drive when I'm upset and need to calm myself. I might drive for as few as twenty minutes or as long as two hours. Tonight was going to be a long one. With every twist and turn of the road, my anger increased in direct proportion to my sadness for Adam. How many men are out there living Adam's hell, too traumatized or poverty stricken to even think of fighting back?

I felt sad for Adam because one of his greatest qualities also happened to be his biggest downfall–he trusted people. Trusting his wife had left him in financial ruin. He had trusted his lawyers, who had tugged on his emotional heartstrings and convinced him to give them his money in the belief that they could get him more time with his son than the standard.

I'd watched Bill fight the same losing battle to keep his children in his life. His emotions and words, long since put to rest after his death, were finding new life in Adam's words and in my heart. How many men are out there fighting this same legal battle to claim victory for their children in a modern-day version of David versus Goliath? I was determined to find out.

Driving down those darkened roads, I thought back to the telephone conversation I had had with my ex, and how he had said "the script doesn't change much" when it comes to divorce. I wanted to believe that we live in a democratic society here in Canada, not under a dictatorship. However, everything I'd seen happen to the men I care about was opposite to the truth–a truth I desperately wanted to believe in.

One of my favourite authors, Dr. Wayne Dyer, said, "Don't die with your music in you." Because of Adam's words tonight, I knew that my song was going to be that book. I also learned that once you realize what your life purpose is, you are changed forever. You can never go back. With awareness comes responsibility, and it had now become my responsibility to use my words to let men know that not all women are against them and that, soon, the world will stand up and take note of their plight.

It was time to go home. The drive had served its purpose, and now there was work to do. I walked into the house and sat in front of my computer before I even took my jacket off. I was excited and scared at the same time–excited because I was finally going to take all of the experiences I'd gone through and do something good with them, but scared because I'd never written a book before. Was I crazy thinking I could do this? I'm passionate, but that doesn't mean that I'm a writer. Part of me wanted to phone Adam and tell him that I'd bitten off more than I could chew. Lucky for me, I have a nagging conscience that always makes me do the right thing. It kept telling me, "At the end of your life, as you take your last breath and God asks you what you did to help your fellow man, what will you answer?"

Once I knew that I wouldn't turn back, I had to face the fear of the unknown. I had no idea of how bad it could get for divorced men or what I was getting myself into. I turned on my computer and typed in the words "Men's Activists" on Google. I felt like Alice in Wonderland, going down the rabbit hole. Like her, I didn't know how deep the hole was or what waited for me at the bottom.

It had been a long day, so I was just going to visit a few sites to get an idea of what issues divorced men continually face, then go to bed. I had no idea that I was only seconds away from hitting the bottom. Moments after pressing the Enter key, I was staring face-to-face with the end of a man's life. Adam had talked to me about his feelings of sheer desperation to stop the harassment, but this poor man had taken that final step. I asked God to comfort him as I read his words out loud. The tears flowed stronger with each word I read.

To whom it may concern: Last Friday (13-October, 1995) my bank account was garnished. I was left with a total of $00.43 in the bank. At this time I have rent and bills to pay which would come to somewhere approaching $1500.00 to $1800.00. Since my last pay was also direct deposited on Friday, I now have no way of supporting myself. I have no money for food or gas for my car to enable me to work. My employer also tells me that they will only pay me by direct deposit. Therefore, I no longer have a job, since the money does not reach me. I

have tried talking to the Family Support people but their answer was: "we have a court order," repeated several times.

I have tried talking to the welfare office, but since I earned over $520.00 last month I am not eligible for assistance. I have had no contact with my daughter in approx. 4 years. I do not even know if she is alive and well. I have tried to keep her informed of my current telephone number but she has never bothered to call. I have no family and no friends, very little food, no viable job and very poor future prospects. I have therefore decided that there is no point in continuing my life. It is my intention to drive to a secluded area near my home, feed exhaust into the car, take some sleeping pills and use the remaining gas in the car to end my life. I would have preferred to die with more dignity. It is my last will and testament that this letter be published for all to see and read. Andrew T. Renouf.

I sat in stunned silence, unable to fully comprehend what I had just read. A man who had had hopes and dreams, who had once loved and laughed, was gone. He hadn't deserved this. What kind of a system have we created where death is easier for a man to take than life? Adam was right–this is hell. Is there any goodness left in people?

The words "I would have preferred to die with more dignity" haunted my thoughts long after I shut down my computer. I prayed for Mr. Renouf that night as I lay staring at the ceiling. As a woman, the loudest message that suicide note conveyed to me was that men feel. We teach men to not show their feelings, but men can and do feel as deeply as any woman. As a mother, the fact that he hadn't seen his daughter in years and that he had died alone was deplorable to me. Issues should never determine the access that children have with their parents, unless some type of abuse is clearly evident. I wanted him to know that he hadn't died in vain and that, because of people like him, I would fight for men's rights and not stop researching and writing until this book was done.

It's amazing what passion does for the soul. I probably slept a total of four hours that night, but I woke up with the energy to move mountains. The girls wanted to go for a walk as a family, but I told them their plans would have to wait until the afternoon, as I had important work to do on the computer. I explained all the events of the night before and my new found sense of purpose. Much to my surprise, they all hugged me, telling me how proud they were of me. They thanked me for how easy I had made their transition through divorce by maintaining a good friendship with their father. I was touched by their words and also proud of my ex and myself. We were working hard to show our daughters that falling out of love doesn't necessarily have to mean falling out of friendship, and it seemed to be working.

I rarely talk to my children about work. I've always tried to maintain good boundaries between my work and home life, but I felt compelled this time to let them know what can happen if both parents don't work together to maintain a healthy environment for the children. I told them how, as a psychiatric nurse, I was often the first face many children saw as they entered our facility with self-inflicted injuries. These youngsters were unyielding in their belief that they were victims of their parents' divorce. Our facility became a revolving door, especially for our female patients, with readmissions commonplace right into their adulthoods. The victim mentality would strengthen as these young girls matured into women and often led to diagnoses of personality disorder, where anger and blame towards others ruled their lives.

When I worked in addiction and then crisis counselling, the same themes played out. Women would usually blame their issues of low self-esteem, self-abuse, or thoughts of suicide on the divorce of their parents in childhood. When I asked them what they were going to do to help themselves, they would often burst into fits of anger, and blame their parents for everything that had gone wrong in their lives since childhood.

I've often wondered how different the lives of damaged children, including those who are eventually diagnosed with a personality disorder, could have been had our courts been willing to adopt a non-adversarial approach where shared and equal parenting is the norm rather than the exception. If children were given equal access to both parents love throughout their lives, I believe that the majority of these children would become well-adjusted adults within society. Children should never be forced to take the side of one parent over the other or be used like pawns in a game of chess.

Our divorce system frustrates me because our government somehow believes it has everything right. It must, because nothing ever changes. Year after year, women still get rich, men still get poor, and the best interests of our children get lost in the fight. Maybe less focus on the financial support of women and more on the emotional support of our children would help empty some of the beds in our psychiatric wards. After twenty years on the healthcare front line, I'm doubtful.

CHAPTER NINETEEN

The first activist for men's rights that I connected with on the Internet was Jeremy Swanson, who runs Fathers Can in Ottawa, Ontario. He is a wealth of street-wise legal knowledge, as well as a prime example of how bad things can get for a divorced man in Canada. Until 2001, he had the type of life that many would envy. He was a highly successful employee at the Canadian War Museum. He had dedicated his life helping to preserve Canadian history and, in 1995, he received word that he'd been nominated to receive the Order of Canada. He had a beautiful home, three wonderful children, and a loving wife—the perfect life, or so he thought. His divorce, which he didn't see coming, has been full of more twists and turns than a good suspense novel, though the ending to his story isn't one that even he could have predicted.

Gone now is the house, the car, the good job, and even his children, whom he hasn't seen in years. His home is now the YMCA, and his possessions are his computer and the clothes on his back. He lives hand to mouth, not knowing when his next meal will come, yet every-day he reaches out to divorced men who are desperate for some ray of hope within their lives. Through his computer and his words, he comforts and guides these men through the legal system, giving them honest and heartfelt advice, letting them know that there is strength in numbers and that giving up is not an option. He's seen the worst, but he keeps fighting for the equality of men within our judicial system. I was moved by the words in one of his recent e-mails: "They call me a hero, Molly, yet all I am doing is telling the truth! For me the finest reward that I could ask for in the work I do is seeing the gratitude and absolute relief on a man's face when he realizes that I believe him."

It was because of Jeremy's connections with the media that, on October 24, 2008, I got my first taste of how bad things are for divorced men on a global level. That Friday, I was a guest on Tom Young's talk-radio program, which is heard in St. John, Moncton, and Halifax on 88.9. When Tom heard that there was a woman defending men's rights, he jumped at the chance to interview me because, as I would come to learn, this is a rarity in the world of divorce.

The interview was scheduled for forty minutes, but when he introduced the topic of men's rights, the phone board lit up like a Christmas tree. In an unprecedented move, he took calls on this topic for an extra hour of his two-hour show. Jeremy had previously put out a worldwide media alert on the Internet stating that I would be on the radio. People listened to the show on their computers from as far away as Australia, New Zealand, and Africa. Many men calling in would try to tell Tom their story but became overcome with grief, going silent after only a few words. Others would fill the airwaves with tears as they tried to whisper out a simple thank you for what we were trying to accomplish on their behalf.

No matter where they were calling from, the issues never changed. I listened to men who were fighting to get their support payments lowered because they didn't have enough money left to eat. Some had not seen their children, often for years, because of an ex-wife who had arbitrarily decided to deny them access, despite a court order. I heard from grandparents being denied access to their grandchildren and men left homeless because of our divorce laws. I listened as second wives of some of these men agreed that they love their men and would support them yet have lost their life savings trying to help their husbands fight against greedy ex-wives they don't even know.

The radio show reinforced what Adam had said about many divorced men being condemned to a life alone because they are financially chained to their ex-wives. The second wives stated that when a woman decides to marry a divorced man who is paying support, she'd better really love him, because that's all she's going to get. She'd better go into the marriage with her eyes wide open, because as long as the ex-wife is getting everything, the man will never be able to support a new family. You may really love your man, they said, but be prepared to see your children go without, probably forever, before you slip that ring on your finger.

I certainly received a crash course on the "dirty side" of divorce, which men face every day, all over the world. Within hours of the show airing, men desperate for help flooded my e-mail inbox. I had never seen anything like it. As fast as I could respond, more e-mails would pour in. I was soon receiving fifty to one hundred messages per day from men in different provinces, states, and countries, all looking for the same answers: "What are my rights? Can you please help me?" The e-mails all contained the same underlying theme: Separated and divorced men were trying to come to grips with the fact that life, as they knew it, was over.

It was disturbing to read about how many men are taken advantage of by our laws and, more so, by their ex-wives, who once professed to love them. If these women had put as much time and energy into working on their marriages as they do in trying to destroy their former spouse, I bet we'd have a lot more happily married couples out there. These e-mails left me feeling ashamed and embarrassed to be a woman but happy that I was getting the opportunity to help, rather than hurt, these men.

In my enthusiasm to help, I overlooked one big thing. I now realized that men's rights are being decimated worldwide, but I had greatly underestimated the severity of the problem. I had assumed I would be flooded with e-mails for a few weeks, or maybe even a couple of months, but that would be it. That couldn't have been further from the truth. I began having trouble finding the time to respond to all the e-mails while working full time. Talk about a global issue! I kept telling myself that I owed it to these men to at least try. Most nights, I would sit at my computer from dinnertime until one or two in the morning typing responses, only to discover that another batch had found its way into my inbox while I slept.

At times, I felt helpless, like I was swimming against the tide. I'm only one person, limited in how much I can help when my only method of communication is my computer. It's frustrating to know that so many of these men need ongoing counselling to move beyond their trauma, yet they have no money to pay for the help they need. I feel guilty contacting these men from the comfort of my warm house when I knew that a lot of them have been homeless or soon will be. It infuriates me that the only network of shelters developed across Canada are for abused women, leaving financially and emotionally abused men to fend for themselves in the streets of our cities. If this is how government treats its citizens and we accept this behaviour without question, just remember that someday, the person in need might be someone you love. Who knows, it might even be you.

Take, for example, this e-mail from Charles:

For the past two years I have been homeless. I have lived in the back of my Suburban and camped for six months. I have also lived in a camper trailer for seven months with no electricity or heat in the winter, and no place to cook. Several times I have gone for days without food. I have lost virtually everything I worked hard for in life. I have struggled with suicidal thoughts and had my licence suspended by maintenance enforcement, costing me my employment. I have had 100% of my employment insurance garnisheed for child support payments I cannot afford, leaving me no money to live on.

I doubt his plight ever garnished any media attention. If I had gone through what he did and our government treated a poverty-stricken woman that way, I wonder how many heads would roll before the media backlash subsided. How could anyone read Charles's words and not be moved to action? And it's not just the words that connect me; it's the honesty and raw emotion that is buried within the text.

One man told me, "Since this all started, I have lost most of the joy of life I used to have. I've been thrust into a world of pain and suffering the likes of which I never imagined in my wildest dreams. The enormous feeling of injustice that consumes me inside is almost paralysing. To call this the justice system is a mockery to the word 'justice.' I'm only alive right now because I know in my heart that being alive is better for my children."

To say that I am angered by what I read each day is an understatement. How can I not be angry when the operative words that define our family law legal system are "insanity" and "apathy" with a good dose of "gender bias" thrown in for good measure?

I'd like to believe that there is an advocate within each of us, waiting to be awakened. I think the late Robert F. Kennedy said it best: "Few have the greatness to bend history; however, each time a man stands up for an ideal, or acts to improve the lot of others, or strikes out against injustice, he sends forth a tiny ripple of hope...and crossing each other from a million different centers of energy and daring those ripples build a current that can sweep down the mightiest walls of oppression and resistance."

His words echo within me each time another desperate e-mail comes across my computer screen. Throughout the process of writing this book, five words keep gripping my heart: "How bad can it get?"

Well, I'll tell you. You're about to find out.

CHAPTER TWENTY

How bad can it get? Meet Ben from Toronto. He was sentenced to jail for ninety days. His crime was that he simply ran out of money with which to pay spousal support payments. The interesting part of this story is following the chain of events which led to the "creation" of a so-called deadbeat dad by our own divorce system. His story is a testament to the ease with which any divorced man can be catapulted into poverty and jail through manipulation of the system by lawyers, judges, ex-wives, and agencies such as the Family Responsibility Office, the FRO.

Ben separated from his wife in 1999. At the time, they had two children, a daughter age seven, and a boy age two. They created a shared-parenting arrangement of two weeks on-two weeks off with each parent that worked beautifully. Now fast forward two and a half years. Ben started dating and became intimate with a new girlfriend who told him that she was on the pill so he didn't have to worry about using contraception. She came back to him six months after they broke up, saying she was pregnant. His youngest daughter was born in

November 2002. Ben then made a visitation agreement with his ex-girlfriend similar to what he had created with his former wife so that his two older children could have a good relationship with his youngest. He and his ex-girlfriend also signed a court-sanctioned financial agreement in which he would pay her three hundred dollars per month until January 2004. This is where the manipulation begins.

In April of 2003, Ben was served with court papers saying that his ex-girlfriend wanted out of the agreement they had signed! I know what you're thinking. That is a legal binding agreement; she doesn't have a leg to stand on. Well, read on. I think your faith in any type of marriage agreement will be quickly shattered. In the spring of 2004, the judge ruled that the agreement they had signed would be thrown out because the three hundred dollar-per month payment Ben was making for his youngest daughter was not in line with the federal child support guidelines. The judge ordered him to pay an extra six hundred dollars per month, retroactive to when his ex-girlfriend had first served him papers, leaving him eight thousand dollars in arrears with principle and interest. The order wasn't based on his present income, but on his income from before his youngest was even born, an income which had been substantially higher. The judge, in making her ruling, completely ignored his financial responsibility to his two older children. By February, Ben could no longer afford a lawyer and had to represent himself in court.

When Ben attempted to get his support payments lowered, the judge lowered them to six hundred and seventy dollars per month plus one hundred towards the arrears, even though he could only afford to pay about two hundred dollars per month. Even though his support was lowered, he was ordered to pay her court costs of four thousand dollars, now leaving him in arrears of twelve thousand dollars. Soon after, the FRO applied and was successful in suspending his driver's license for being in arrears, even though the judge was fully aware that Ben couldn't earn more than a minimal income without his car because of his line of work.

In January of 2006, the FRO was after Ben again, this time asking the judge for a jail term. At that time, the judge told Ben to keep up with spousal support payments, which, because of his income drop, were now based on three times his actual income, plus payback arrears, which were sitting at ten thousand dollars. In his e-mail to me, Ben states, **"It began to feel to me like the unstated message is willfully walk away from your children, and the pain we are administering will go away. I had no intention of doing so. I am also thinking, why this judge even is bothering to prolong the inevitable."**

The inevitable eventually came. In the summer of 2006, Ben was sentenced to ninety days in jail. He was then handcuffed by the court security and taken downstairs, where he was stripped, searched, and processed for the trip to jail. According to Ben, while in jail, he was in a cell with two other guys, one for assault and one for armed robbery. Within the same cell block, there were people charged with dealing drugs and murder. Ben told me in his e-mail that the men he was bunked with were glad that there were three to his cell, because every day of their sentence would equate to 3 days being served. Ben said that he also found out that this is a luxury provided only to people like drug dealers, murders, rapists, or armed robbers. It does not apply to fathers who fell behind on support payments.

The positive component to Ben's story is his family. His family raised ten thousand dollars to pay his bail so he could get out of jail in time to attend his thirteen year-old daughter's grade 8 graduation. Unfortunately, a month later, the FRO was back on his doorstep with another request to put him back in jail for ninety days because he was still so far behind on his support payments. At the time of this e-mail, he was once again appealing his support order. Provinces will not release data on annual incarcerations of defaulters, but Canadian Divorce Information conservatively estimates the number is from two thousand to three thousand annually.

I recently contacted Ben and told him that I was writing this book. I asked him to give me his thoughts on what he would like people to know after all he's been through. These are his words:

The injustice and the shattering of my belief system will never leave me. I will never be the same again. Family Law tortures men slowly, making sure it is as long and painful a death as possible. This is torture well beyond anything that has taken place in history. I spent 36 years of my life with nothing more than a speeding ticket, and at age 40 I was sent to jail for not having money. Going to jail I thought of how ridiculous this was, and coming out I realized that murderers, drug dealers and child molesters receive more leniency than a father does from this system.

After you come to the realization that your life is not likely to get much better, and that the time that you've lost can never be regained, it is virtually impossible to go through a day without those thoughts being on your mind. It makes every aspect of your day ten times harder than it seemed before, and keeping your spirits high or your initiative to succeed, becomes extremely difficult. In short, nothing you were before will be again, and all that is lost, will never return. When I say this I am not talking dollars and cents, I am talking about your being, your soul, and everything that used to define you as a human being.

Approximately 72,000 divorces occur in Canada annually. This means that only about two to four percent of the fathers who are behind in their support payments actually go to jail, but the fact still remains that in a democratic society, this shouldn't happen at all. You may be asking yourself, if jail is an infrequently used punishment against men, then what is the punishment of choice? By far, statements of accusation hurled in court by the ex-wife against her former spouse is the method of choice for maximal damage to the man's reputation and character in the shortest period of time. From all of the e-mails I've read, this tactic seems to be used most often when the ex-wife wants sole custody of the children and fears that her ex-husband may fight her on this issue. The allegations usually claim physical, emotional, or sexual abuse by the husband against his wife, children, or both. The man is left to prove his innocence in court, rather than the ex proving his guilt, which makes court a very stressful place for the man to be, especially if the allegations involve sexual abuse against a child. Just ask Brad. He's been through it.

Brad e-mailed me with his story. He told me that his ex-wife was so abusive that it was affecting their two-year-old son. According to Brad, the abusive behavior got so bad that his son would take him by the hand, walk into his bedroom, and shut the door, and say, "It's OK, Daddy, now we can play." All the while, his ex would stand outside the bedroom door, yelling, "Now look what you have done!" like it was his fault that their son had retreated to the safety of his bedroom. When Brad had told her that he wanted out of the marriage, she had taken off with their son and gone to a women's transition house. According to Brad, she didn't get every-thing she wanted, which was to completely cut him out of his son's life, so she made sexual abuse allegations, against him, with their son.

In Brad's own words:

In short I have been accused of everything by her and have proven all of her allegations to be false. She has received no reprimand for any of the false allegations she alleged, or for refusing me access to my own son, four times, despite a court order. I have cried for days with no sleep. I couldn't eat or even leave my house. I wanted to die because the pain was so great, but I knew how much my son loves me. I talked, cried and yelled to both friends and counselors. It has been three years and I'm still in court. I've lost all my jobs, been lied to by judges and I continue to be abused by the court system. I am still fighting for my boy. All I've ever wanted is 50/50

time with my son, but I don't have that yet. I keep fighting for my son's right to have equal parenting.

I am a mess and my whole life has been destroyed. I'm not sure what the future holds. Police, Doctors and Counselors are all aware of women who do the things my ex has done. They all nod yes as soon as I start talking and tell me how I'm not the first, and won't be the last. The sad part is that nobody does anything about it.

I was a youth worker with high risk youth, and I worked with Developmentally Disabled people. I was hired during all of this to work for a school board with special needs kids. Needless to say, I never even went to work there for one day, because there was no way I could look after other children when the court and my ex were trying to take my own son away. I still have my hiring papers, including my employee number.

I am on Welfare now, still suffering from the ongoing sickness that festers in our family court, and within society, in regards to the best interest of our children. What a joke it all seems sometimes. Please don't stop fighting for the best interests of our children, especially with you being a woman Molly!

Never underestimate the tenacity of a vindictive ex-wife or the insanity of family law. This next e-mail takes the persistence of using sexual allegations to get what you want to a whole new level. This is David's story:

My story is painful. I am the guy that about 20 years ago won sole custody of my twins, a boy and a girl, both aged two, after a 13 day trial in Texas. I was fighting against their pediatrician mother who was accusing me of sexually abusing my children in my hometown. After 10 years of sole custody, and with my children thriving, she goes back into court in another state, and the judge gives her sole custody, without any hearing or presentation of evidence, whatsoever. She basically hired an inside attorney, and the whole thing was over for me in thirty days.

Seven years later I am alienated from the children I raised, and went to hell and back for. My ex-wife, being a pediatrician, had the financial resources, and spent over $250,000, over almost two decades of litigation, in three states. I should write a book as the events in my case are almost surreal. But I know better than to say that, because there is no end to the evil and destruction Family Law can bring to innocent parents. Unfortunately, there is always a worse case than your own, and they are all personally very painful. So we fight...

As with Brad and David's stories, allegations of sexual or physical harm, especially to a child, are generally the kiss of death for the man. How is the ex-husband supposed to defend himself when it's his word against hers, especially within a female-oriented court system? If the allegations are true, then by all means, get the man out of the picture quickly, but if they are lies and the woman knows it, then that is the sickest form of abuse imaginable that can be perpetrated against a father. In such a case, I believe the woman involved should face criminal prosecution and lose custody of her children to the father permanently.

I talked earlier in the book about parental alienation syndrome, with what Rick and Adam went through. Once again, in the context of child custody, it is the programming of a child by one parent into a campaign of denigration against the other parent, without justification and is used by parents, generally women, to gain control of their children.

While writing this book, I attended a special forum on this topic. When the moderator called on men to ask the guest speaker a question, the men often had trouble containing their emotions, as a lot of them hadn't seen their children in years.

It is one thing to talk about alienation, but it is another thing for an adult to come forward and describe the negative impact it has had on his or her life. Once you read Craig's story, you will never question the horrific impact of this phenomenon, ever again, on our children. This is an e-mail that Craig sent to his good friend Jeremy, of Fathers Can, in Ottawa. On this particular day, Jeremy was hurting, because it was his son's birthday and the end of another year without seeing his son, whom he loves very much. Jeremy was kind enough to send me this e-mail.

My mom suffered from mental illness. I was taken from my dad when I was 5 years old. I'm now 45. I never saw my father again. At 43, in the midst of my own divorce nightmare I found out that he had died of brain cancer in 1996. I always loved him even though my mom played the Parental Alienation Syndrome card. For years I hated him! Unfortunately, I was brainwashed. My mom settled for $2500.00. She signed off, end of story.

My life ended up being worth $100.00 per year for 18 years. I never saw any of the money. She partied for a while until it was gone, and then nothing changed in our lives.

I just want you to know, that no matter what P.A.S. garbage I was fed, I eventually figured it out. My Dad was a good guy, probably similar to you and me. I somehow ended up in his hometown of Sudbury. I looked up his obituary. It said that his second wife and step-kids loved him dearly. I met strangers who said to me, "You related to Brian?" I said, "yeah." These people emitted a loving feeling to me. You know Jeremy; I sensed the love my dad had for me right from the beginning. No one, no political garbage, no nothing can change that. Your children will one day know your love. They will! I am them! There's a love that that no corrupt law, or political movement, or anything can deny. They will search for you in the years to come, mark my words.

Divorce is now a worldwide epidemic, on a scale that rivals AIDS or world hunger. In the case of AIDS or starvation, the symptoms are physical; they have been intensively documented and can be easily recognized. If the symptoms are caught early enough and treated properly, the person may well live a full and productive life. But the problem with divorce is that the symptoms aren't as much physical as they are emotional. And how do you cure an emotion? For a man, divorce is, if not a death sentence, at best a life sentence. It's treatable, but not curable. It is what I call "the silent killer." What tests can you run to come up with a diagnosis of a broken heart, after a father has been effectively removed from his child's life or is forced into having supervised visits, even though he has done nothing wrong in the eyes of the law to even deserve this? What pill do you give a father to stop the tears, after his own child looks him straight in the eye and says, "I never want to see you again" after some backroom manipulation by his ex-wife? What antibiotic do you give a father to help him when his soul is dying because he is without his children? And believe me, men do die.

Just read the words of Jean-Marc Bessette, a divorced father who went on a hunger strike in Rimouski while I was writing this book to protest the lack of public funding for men who are divorced, as compared to women:"Four men commit suicide every day in Quebec, with two or three of them being fathers undergoing separation or divorce. This stems in part from stresses due to divorce and being deprived of their children. Children need their father."

How many fathers have to die before we finally wake up and realize that fostering an environment where women are allowed to harass men to the brink of death is not in the best interests of our children? I wouldn't want to be the one to tell my child that their father's dead because I put more value on money than on his life or the relationship he had with his child. And imagine when my child looks up at me with tears in his eyes and says, "But I miss Daddy"; do you really think he'll care how much money divorce gave me?

Maybe it's time as women that we ask ourselves, "Whose best interests are we really fighting for?" Be honest with yourself. If it's not the children, then maybe it's time to make better choices, because everyone loses out when a child grows up without a father. I was about to learn that lesson firsthand, from a most unlikely source–my daughter.

CHAPTER TWENTY-ONE

"Mom, come here quick!" my daughter yelled from the next room. "You're not going to believe this. I just found Bill's kids on Facebook."

I thought I must have heard her wrong. I hadn't seen Bill's children in nine years, but when I sat down in front of Anne's computer, there were his two oldest girls, though I hardly recognized them. I remembered those little girls I'd fallen in love with, the ones with the ponytails and chubby cheeks, squealing with laughter as their father playfully rode them on his back. Looking at them now with sunken eyes, hollow cheeks, and flat, expressionless stares broke my heart. They wrote on their respective sites about the sadness in their lives, their struggles with drugs, and the hope that they would someday find their way in the world. It made me wonder if their lives would have taken a different turn had Bill been alive to guide them and help them grow up.

In Adam's case, it wasn't death, but rather parental alienation, that had cheated him out of the ability to be a father. The result was the same, however– two more victims claimed. A young boy who once loved his father has been replaced by a spoiled child taught to value money more than his father, and a wonderful man with so much love to give has been silenced. With each passing month, Adam's memory of what it feels like to be a father, to hear his child's laugh, or to simply hold his sons hand is slowly fading into obscurity.

In his own life, Adam fought hard to survive but eventually lost everything: his house, his business, and, worst of all, his child. This once-successful dentist who, like my cousin Rick, had basically given up everything to his ex-wife, was left with no other option but to go to legal-aid for help. There was no way he could continue paying huge support payments and hope to even feed himself. His only option was to get back to court and have a judge lower his monthly payments by writing up a new support order. Without legal aid, he couldn't do it, as hiring a lawyer was out of the question.

But legal aid wouldn't give him the time of day. They turned him down because he had made too much money the previous year to qualify. The fact that he was currently bankrupt was irrelevant in the eyes of the law. This meant that no matter what job he might get, even one at minimum wage, he would have all his pay garnisheed monthly because his original support order still stated that he was making a six-figure gross income.

Adam would have been homeless and on the street if it hadn't been for the kindness of a dear friend, who took him in, put a roof over his head, fed him, and asked nothing in return. That's good, because Adam had nothing left to give other than his gratitude. He's scared because he doesn't know if he can escape an eventual life on the streets. As soon as he makes money, the government scoops it up for back support he owes. Even if he can get welfare, he wonders if he can survive after his ex takes her cut.

Depression has become Adam's constant companion, a daily reminder of how far he has fallen from the life he once knew. He has reached out for help, but his attempts have been in vain. Adam's an educated man and knows he needs help, and he's willing to do the work to get himself back on his feet again, but he keeps asking, "Where is the help?" Adam describes the looks he gets from people out in the community as nothing short of bewilderment when he starts asking where the men's shelters are or if he can get a list of all the social services available for men going through divorce. He's said to me, "When you're a man going through divorce, you go it alone, and I do mean alone!"

Ironically, the only people who have consistently been there for Adam during his ordeal are other divorced dads. As Adam says, "Thank God you don't need government funding to give another displaced father a hug, because if you did, all would be lost for men."

Then there's my cousin Rick. I wonder how his life would have been different if his ex-wife hadn't turned the kids' hearts against him. I remember him talking with pride when his children were young and how much he looked forward to watching them grow up. The thought of watching his children graduate from school, get married, and start families of their own had brought a smile to his face. If someone mentioned the idea of him becoming a grandfather someday he'd be beside himself. He could talk for an hour of how he was going to spoil the future little ones rotten. He was so full of life and had so much love to give back then.

With all he has gone through, he still loves his children, but they don't love him back. His children never recovered from the effects of the parental alienation. Rick hasn't seen his son or daughter in nearly ten years. He tries to be optimistic, never losing hope that one day they will call so he can tell them about the father they never got a chance to know. Here is a man who worked his whole life and gave almost every penny he ever made to his ex-wife. He now is just free of her, eighteen years post-divorce, because she finally agreed to stop making him pay support–but only after he paid her off by cashing in the last of his retirement investments worth twenty thousand dollars.

My cousin's supposed golden years are anything but golden. He and his second wife still live in the small apartment I mentioned with the high-level security, because neither of them can move beyond the paranoia that someone is out there, beyond those doors and locks, waiting to hurt them. Rick has become a recluse. He trusts no one. Now, he simply exists.

I found out in the midst of writing this chapter that Rick has been diagnosed with cancer, an aggressive and often fatal form that attacks the pleural membrane surrounding the lungs. The doctors have told him that long-term exposure to asbestos is the most common cause for this type of cancer. They've told him that intervention such as chemotherapy, radiation, and surgery may help to extend his life but that the overall prognosis is poor. For the first time in eighteen years, this man had finally found peace within his life. Now he is forced to deal with his own mortality.

I had a chance meeting with my cousin's wife in a parking lot a while back as I was out running errands. She saw me, waved, and gestured me towards her car. When I got there, Rick was sitting quietly in the passenger seat. He looked tired from all the medical tests he'd gone through. When he saw me, he grabbed my arm and pulled me toward him so we could talk. His voice was weak, his breathing laboured, but his words that day were powerful and to the point. "Molly, I didn't get a chance to tell you this earlier but just after I was diagnosed with cancer, a bailiff served me with court papers. My children are suing me once again for supposedly stealing their college-fund money some twenty years ago. Get this book written! Men have to know that the harassment never ends. It's when you let your guard down and allow yourself the luxury of feeling safe that the nightmare resurfaces. You know, in some ways, when death comes, it's going to be a blessing. I'll finally be free of all this hell that family law and my own family keep putting me through. Please let me know that my life and death had meaning. If that book helps even one man to avoid the suffering I went through, I'll be grateful."

And to think, we do all of this "in the best interests of the children."

FINAL THOUGHTS

The system of family law that our governments have created is broken and needs to be fixed. Most judges are ill-trained to deal with modern-day issues such as parental alienation or stay-at-home fathers who are seeking custody of their children. Our legal system is slow to embrace the changing face of today's family unit. Single-parent households are no longer viewed as the exception, and women are entering the workforce in record numbers.

Judges need to realize that the era of the stay-at-home mom is over, and decisions made concerning child-custody issues must be based on something more substantial than a person's gender. In two-parent families, both spouses tend to have jobs outside the home and work long hours. This has forced both parents to take on responsibilities that in the past were carried out based on gender. Within today's legal system, men have no value. The courts don't recognize the importance of a father in a child's life or the strides father's have made in the area of child rearing over the past few decades. No matter how hard men try, they can't shake the stereotype imposed on them by family law that they are second-class parents.

According to David Blankenhorn, author of Fatherless America: Confronting Our Most Urgent Social Problem: "Fatherlessness is the most harmful demographic trend of this generation. It is the leading cause of declining child well-being in our society. It is also the engine driving our most urgent social problems from crime to adolescent pregnancy to child sexual abuse to domestic violence....Certainly, despite the difficulty of proving causation in the social sciences, the weight of evidence increasingly supports the conclusion that fatherlessness is a primary generator of violence among young men."

According to Barbara Kay of the *National Post* in her July 18, 2008, article "Give Dad a Chance," in ninety percent of litigated custody cases, the mother gains sole custody while the father is left to the generosity of an ex-wife to gain anything close to equal access to his children.

Men looking for support from the government on this issue are in for a big surprise. In the same article, Barbara highlights the failure of the Canadian government to act on its own recommendations concerning custody and access. In the 1998 government report titled "For the Sake of the Children," which took more than a year to compile and included forty eight recommendations, one theme emerged: "Sole custody as it pertains to the majority of custody and access disputes denies children and the non-custodial parent basic human rights, and puts children's psychological and emotional health at risk."

Polls show that eighty percent of Canadians support equal parenting (in the absence of violence) as being fair to parents and best for their children. The Liberal government in power at the time the report came out did nothing but sweep it under the carpet. Stephen Harper's Conservatives haven't done much better. In his 2006 electoral platform, Mr. Harper promised to implement "a presumption of shared parental responsibility unless determined not to be in the best interest of the child," with mediation being another viable option. In a 2007 policy paper by University of British Columbia's sociology professor Edward Kruk, Canada's foremost expert in custody issues, Professor Kruk provided overwhelming peer-reviewed data supporting "shared parental responsibility." His findings included "that a child must spend at least 40% of their time with a parent in order to maintain a beneficial attachment."

There is some light at the end of the tunnel. Saskatoon-Wanuskewin Conservative MP Maurice Vellacott has been working in parliament to get his private members bill (C-422) on shared equal parenting passed into law. As of fall 2009, his bill is still working its way through the governmental hierarchy.

Government statistics indicate that a disproportionate amount of Canadian taxpayer dollars is being spent on shelters for abused women, even though men as well as women pay into the same tax pool. In 2005-2006, Canada budgeted three hundred seventy-seven million dollars to help support approximately five hundred fifty women's shelters. During that same time period, Canada's budget for the one privately run men's shelter in Alberta was zero.

So, gentlemen, if you are trying to get custody of your child, or that elusive fifty-fifty split of your hard-earned assets in court, please realize that the cards are stacked against you. The courts aren't male-friendly, and neither is the government. At least you can take comfort in knowing that you're not crazy. You were right all along. The laws aren't fair, and don't let anyone tell you otherwise.

Most likely, you'll end up paying child and spousal support, your ex will get custody of your child, and your visitation with your kids will be every other week-end and one evening during the week. That is unless you have bags of money to throw away on court costs, years of free time to fight, and a total disregard for the future of your own health. Remember, I talked to hundreds of men just like you to write this book. Learn from their misfortunes.

What I will do is share with you the lessons I learned while writing this book. I can't stop you from having to go through this horrible process called divorce, but I can give you tips that may help to minimize the damage you incur along the way.

The first thing you need to know is that if you and your wife signed a pre-nuptial agreement before you got married and you think your assets are protected, think again. All of the divorced men I talked to who had these agreements drawn up said that they never stood up to a challenge in court. Many judges simply disregarded them. In other instances, the ex-wife was able to get the agreement thrown out simply by saying that she was pressured into signing or never understood the agreement.

Statistically, it's more likely that the wife will approach the husband and ask for a divorce. Once you have been told that your marriage is over, you will feel countless emotions, including anger, sadness, and fear. The most important thing here is that you think logically and keep your emotions in check, not only that first day, but every day afterwards! The courts are funny. If a woman rants and raves, her outbursts are considered justified because of the stress she is under, but if a man exhibits the same behavior, he is viewed as unstable. Don't give your ex-wife's lawyer any ammunition with which to make you look bad in court.

When it comes to legal representation, don't be too quick to hire the first lawyer you come across in the phone book. If the lawyer you pick works for a large firm, just remember that someone has to help pay for all those plush chairs and fancy offices. Interview a number of lawyers before you make your final decision. During the interview, make the lawyer aware of how much you can afford to spend on legal fees, and what your goals are in going to court. A good lawyer will be up-front and honest with you and tell you right from the start if your expectations are realistic or even attainable on your budget.

Make sure that the lawyer you pick is a good listener and is genuinely interested in helping you obtain a fair settlement. If they are focused more on your money than on you, run away while you still can. I stressed this next point in the book, but it's worth repeating: Your lawyer is not your friend, never was, and never will be. Whether you win or lose is of no consequence to them, because either way, they get paid. Lawyers don't get rich in calm waters; they make money from conflict and drama. Always make your decisions based on logic and not when you are emotional. If you act, instead of re-acting, you have a better chance of keeping some of your money.

If you and your ex are on good terms, I recommend that you seek out a good paralegal. As I said in the book, the total cost of our divorce was less than one thousand dollars.

During a divorce, your children are the priority, so never allow them to be used as bargaining chips. This divorce is between you and your spouse, so keep the children out of it. I don't care how much you dislike each other; no one should ever badmouth a mother or a father in front of a child. Children are born with an innate desire to love both parents. Don't brainwash them into choosing one parent over another. Think about it–as a child, would you have wanted your parents to do that to you?

Try to resolve your divorce issues quickly before emotions get flared up, the ability to reason flies out the window, and thoughts of revenge begin to creep into the picture. If you were unfortunate enough to marry a spouse with a personality disorder (chapter ten), I can't emphasize this point enough. Don't fight over small material possessions. It doesn't make sense to pay a lawyer four hundred dollars per hour to decide who gets the toaster. Ask yourself this question: "What am I willing to give up so that I secure my freedom, keep my health, and get on with my life?"

This is especially true when it comes to spousal support. I understand a father paying a reasonable amount of support for a child, but spousal support is just the financial gravy train that keeps on giving. Who wouldn't want that nice monthly paycheque for years or maybe life? See if you can get your ex to sign off on spousal support. Her demands may be ridiculous, but if the two of you can meet somewhere in the middle, you'll come out ahead financially in the long run. If you're paying spousal support and you're hoping to get married again in the future, don't forget that your new partner may have to go without because she may be forced to contribute part of her income to support your ex-wife.

If you have that gut feeling that your divorce is going to get ugly right from the word "go," I suggest you listen very closely to what I am about to tell you. Any communication that you have with your ex in written form is admissible in court as evidence and can be used against you. This includes journals, notes, answering-machine messages, text messages, and e-mails. Always assume that a lawyer is listening to your conversations as well as reading and analyzing everything you write. Remember that, and you will be less likely to express emotions that could come back to haunt you later.

Another key to surviving an ugly divorce is simple: DO NOT RESPOND. I can't make it any clearer than that. In this type of divorce, the ex will taunt and bait you. They want to get you so emotionally off centre that you say or do something that they can use against you in court. Don't give them the opportunity. As I always say, "You can't start a war if only one army shows up." If you have to respond to something, keep your answers short and, to the point and only offer up the information you have to by law.

When a divorce gets ugly and child custody is at stake, false allegations often begin to surface in order to discredit the character of the opposing spouse. In these cases, the most common allegation is that of a father sexually or physically abusing his own child. If you are reading this and are concerned that this may happen to you, the best thing you can do to protect yourself is to never allow yourself to be alone with your child without a reputable witness being present. It's sad that we have to think that way, but the most important thing here is that you don't lose access to your child.

Going through divorce is hard enough on your self-esteem, but when you add in attacks on your character or false allegations from an ex who promised to always love you, the pain you feel can be debilitating. The last lesson I will share is that if you want to survive divorce, you have make yourself a priority. Continue to be involved with the activities that made you happy before you got separated. Eat healthy foods and associate with positive people. Talk to someone you trust within your church, a good friend, a therapist who comes highly recommended, or a family member. If you have access to a computer and the Internet, get connected to an activist group in your area. These groups consist of very knowledgeable men and women who are either going through, or have gone through divorce themselves. They will be able to answer a lot of your questions and possibly even save you money on court costs. They are all fighting for family law reform so that one day the needs of all men and women going through divorce will be represented equally and fairly without the gender bias that now exists.

The best way to help facilitate healing after divorce is to turn your negative experience into a positive one. It is estimated that when you go to bed tonight, 1.5 million Canadian children will go to bed without their fathers. Tomorrow, several hundred more dads will be cast from the lives of their children because of family law. Help advocate for shared equal parenting. Help make equal time spent with both parents the new standard rather than the exception. This truly is in the best interest of the children.

The ability to create change is a mindset. It begins with awareness, is fuelled by passion, and is strengthened by faith. Within the pages of this book are seeds of awareness. Pay this book forward. The more seeds we plant, the faster awareness will blossom. Governments don't listen to reason, but if we all remain persistent in our quest, the weight of the truth and the strength of our collective voice will eventually topple the resistance of even the most defiant political power. Will we win this battle for our fathers and children? I believe that the late great Henry Ford said it best: "Whether you think you can or think you can't, either way you are right."

Molly Murphy

ABOUT THE AUTHOR

Molly Murphy is a registered nurse with a specialized designation in psychiatry having more than twenty years experience in the healthcare field. She resides in Ontario with her three daughters, dividing her time between her three passions, with family being her number-one priority. This is followed by working tirelessly to make positive change for seniors through her work as a resource nurse at one of the largest retirement communities in her area as well as being an outspoken activist for family law reform. Her goal in advocating is twofold: to help bring into law reforms that truly reflect the best interest of our children and to create awareness through her writing concerning the dysfunction and discrimination that exists today on a global basis within our family law system.

LaVergne, TN USA
20 May 2010
183346LV00001B/93/P